50 College Student Food Recipes for Home

By: Kelly Johnson

Table of Contents

- Spaghetti with marinara sauce
- Grilled cheese sandwich
- Ramen noodles with egg
- Tuna salad wrap
- Quesadillas
- Chicken stir-fry with vegetables
- Pita bread pizzas
- Veggie fried rice
- BLT sandwich
- Baked potatoes with toppings
- Macaroni and cheese
- Omelette with toast
- Hummus and veggie wraps
- Beef or bean burritos
- Caesar salad with grilled chicken
- Tomato soup with grilled cheese
- Stuffed bell peppers
- Chicken fajitas
- Greek yogurt with granola and fruit
- Pancakes with syrup and fruit
- Caprese salad
- Avocado toast with poached egg
- Quinoa salad with vegetables
- Sloppy Joes
- Spinach and cheese stuffed pasta shells
- Teriyaki chicken bowl with rice
- Chicken Caesar wraps
- Veggie chili
- Pesto pasta with cherry tomatoes
- Tacos with ground beef or beans
- Baked chicken drumsticks
- Pad Thai noodles
- Minestrone soup
- BBQ pulled pork sandwiches
- Shrimp scampi with pasta

- Chicken quesadillas
- Ratatouille
- Eggplant Parmesan
- Sushi rolls (vegetarian or with fish)
- Lentil soup
- Stuffed baked apples
- Falafel wraps
- Baked tilapia with vegetables
- Chicken and vegetable kebabs
- Tortellini with pesto sauce
- Veggie stir-fry noodles
- Tofu tacos
- Lemon garlic shrimp with couscous
- Black bean burgers
- Mushroom risotto

Spaghetti with marinara sauce

Ingredients:

- 8 ounces spaghetti
- 2 tablespoons olive oil
- 3 cloves garlic, minced
- 1 can (28 ounces) crushed tomatoes
- 1 teaspoon dried oregano
- 1 teaspoon dried basil
- 1/2 teaspoon red pepper flakes (optional)
- Salt and pepper to taste
- Fresh basil leaves, chopped (for garnish, optional)
- Grated Parmesan cheese (for serving, optional)

Instructions:

1. Cook the spaghetti according to package instructions until al dente. Drain and set aside.
2. In a large skillet, heat the olive oil over medium heat. Add the minced garlic and sauté for about 1 minute, until fragrant.
3. Stir in the crushed tomatoes, dried oregano, dried basil, and red pepper flakes (if using). Season with salt and pepper to taste.
4. Simmer the marinara sauce for about 10-15 minutes, stirring occasionally, until it thickens slightly and the flavors meld together.
5. Add the cooked spaghetti to the skillet with the marinara sauce. Toss to coat the spaghetti evenly with the sauce.
6. Serve hot, garnished with chopped fresh basil leaves and grated Parmesan cheese if desired.

Enjoy your homemade spaghetti with marinara sauce!

Grilled cheese sandwich

Ingredients:

- 2 slices of bread (any type you prefer, such as white, whole wheat, or sourdough)
- Butter, softened
- 2 slices of cheese (cheddar, American, Swiss, or your favorite melting cheese)

Instructions:

1. Heat a non-stick skillet or griddle over medium-low heat.
2. Butter one side of each slice of bread.
3. Place one slice of bread, buttered side down, on the skillet.
4. Add one slice of cheese on top of the bread in the skillet.
5. Place the second slice of bread, buttered side up, on top of the cheese.
6. Cook the sandwich for 2-4 minutes on each side, or until the bread is golden brown and the cheese inside is melted.
7. Carefully flip the sandwich with a spatula and cook the other side until it's golden brown and the cheese is fully melted.
8. Remove the grilled cheese sandwich from the skillet and let it cool for a minute before slicing it diagonally (optional) and serving.

Enjoy your delicious grilled cheese sandwich!

Ramen noodles with egg

Ingredients:

- 1 package of instant ramen noodles (flavor packet optional)
- 1 egg
- Water
- Optional: green onions, sesame seeds, chili oil, or other toppings of your choice

Instructions:

1. Boil Water: Bring a pot of water to a boil. If using the flavor packet from the ramen noodles, you can add it to the boiling water now.
2. Cook Ramen Noodles: Add the ramen noodles to the boiling water and cook according to the package instructions, usually about 2-3 minutes until the noodles are tender.
3. Prepare Egg: While the noodles are cooking, crack an egg into a small bowl or cup. You can beat the egg lightly with a fork if you prefer a more uniform consistency.
4. Add Egg to Noodles: Once the noodles are almost done cooking, lower the heat to medium-low. Slowly pour the beaten egg into the pot of noodles while gently stirring the water with chopsticks or a fork. The egg will cook and form ribbons in the hot water.
5. Finish Cooking: Continue to cook for about 1 minute or until the egg is fully cooked to your liking (some prefer a runny yolk, others prefer it fully cooked).
6. Serve: Remove the pot from heat. Carefully transfer the noodles and egg into a bowl. Garnish with sliced green onions, sesame seeds, a drizzle of chili oil, or any other toppings you like.
7. Enjoy: Stir everything together and enjoy your comforting bowl of ramen noodles with egg!

This recipe is versatile, allowing you to customize it with additional vegetables, meats, or spices to suit your taste preferences.

Tuna salad wrap

Ingredients:

- 1 can (5 ounces) of tuna, drained
- 2 tablespoons mayonnaise
- 1 tablespoon Dijon mustard
- 1/4 cup finely chopped celery
- 1/4 cup finely chopped red onion
- Salt and pepper, to taste
- 2 large flour tortillas (8-10 inches in diameter)
- Lettuce leaves
- Sliced tomatoes (optional)
- Sliced avocado (optional)

Instructions:

1. Prepare Tuna Salad: In a mixing bowl, combine the drained tuna, mayonnaise, Dijon mustard, finely chopped celery, and finely chopped red onion. Mix well until all ingredients are evenly combined. Season with salt and pepper to taste.
2. Assemble Wraps: Lay out the flour tortillas on a clean surface. Place lettuce leaves in the center of each tortilla, leaving space around the edges for folding.
3. Add Tuna Salad: Divide the prepared tuna salad mixture evenly between the two tortillas, spreading it out over the lettuce leaves.
4. Optional Additions: If desired, add sliced tomatoes and/or sliced avocado on top of the tuna salad.
5. Wrap: To wrap each tortilla, fold in the sides first, then roll up tightly from the bottom to enclose the filling.
6. Serve: Cut each wrap in half diagonally (optional) and serve immediately, or wrap tightly in plastic wrap or foil for later.

Enjoy your tuna salad wraps as a satisfying and portable meal option!

Quesadillas

Ingredients:

- 4 large flour tortillas
- 2 cups shredded cheese (cheddar, Monterey Jack, or a blend)
- 1 cup cooked chicken, shredded (optional)
- 1/2 cup diced bell peppers (optional)
- 1/4 cup diced red onion (optional)
- 1/4 cup chopped fresh cilantro (optional)
- 1 teaspoon ground cumin (optional)
- Salt and pepper, to taste
- Cooking oil or butter for frying

Instructions:

1. Prepare the Filling (if using): In a bowl, combine the shredded cheese, cooked chicken (if using), diced bell peppers, diced red onion, chopped cilantro, ground cumin, salt, and pepper. Mix well to evenly distribute the ingredients.
2. Assemble the Quesadillas: Lay out two tortillas on a clean surface. Divide the cheese mixture evenly between the two tortillas, spreading it out to cover the entire surface. Optionally, add other fillings like chicken, beans, or spinach.
3. Top with Another Tortilla: Place another tortilla on top of each cheese-covered tortilla to create two quesadilla sandwiches.
4. Cook the Quesadillas: Heat a large skillet or griddle over medium heat. Add a small amount of cooking oil or butter to coat the bottom of the skillet.
5. Carefully place one quesadilla in the skillet and cook for about 2-3 minutes on each side, or until the tortilla is golden brown and crispy, and the cheese inside is melted.
6. Repeat: If your skillet is large enough, you can cook both quesadillas at the same time. Otherwise, cook them one at a time.
7. Serve: Once cooked, transfer the quesadillas to a cutting board and let them cool for a minute. Cut each quesadilla into wedges using a sharp knife or pizza cutter.
8. Optional Garnishes: Serve quesadillas hot with sour cream, salsa, guacamole, or any other toppings you prefer.

Enjoy your homemade quesadillas as a tasty snack or meal!

Chicken stir-fry with vegetables

Ingredients:

- 2 boneless, skinless chicken breasts, thinly sliced
- 2 tablespoons soy sauce
- 1 tablespoon oyster sauce (optional)
- 1 tablespoon cornstarch
- 1/2 teaspoon ground black pepper
- 2 tablespoons vegetable oil, divided
- 2 cloves garlic, minced
- 1 inch piece of ginger, minced or grated
- 1 onion, thinly sliced
- 1 bell pepper (any color), thinly sliced
- 1 cup broccoli florets
- 1 carrot, thinly sliced
- 1/2 cup snow peas or snap peas
- Salt, to taste
- Cooked rice or noodles, for serving

Instructions:

1. Marinate the Chicken: In a bowl, combine the thinly sliced chicken breasts with soy sauce, oyster sauce (if using), cornstarch, and ground black pepper. Mix well and let it marinate for at least 15-20 minutes.
2. Heat the Wok or Skillet: Heat 1 tablespoon of vegetable oil in a large wok or skillet over medium-high heat.
3. Cook the Chicken: Add the marinated chicken to the hot wok or skillet, spreading it out in a single layer. Cook for 3-4 minutes, stirring occasionally, until the chicken is cooked through and lightly browned. Remove the chicken from the wok and set aside.
4. Cook the Vegetables: In the same wok or skillet, add the remaining 1 tablespoon of vegetable oil. Add minced garlic and ginger, and stir-fry for about 30 seconds until fragrant.
5. Add sliced onion, bell pepper, broccoli florets, carrot, and snow peas to the wok. Stir-fry for 4-5 minutes, or until the vegetables are tender-crisp.
6. Combine and Season: Return the cooked chicken to the wok with the vegetables. Stir everything together and cook for another 1-2 minutes to heat through. Taste and adjust seasoning with salt if needed.
7. Serve: Serve the chicken stir-fry immediately over cooked rice or noodles.

Enjoy your flavorful and nutritious chicken stir-fry with vegetables!

Pita bread pizzas

Ingredients:

- Pita bread rounds (whole wheat or white)
- Pizza sauce or marinara sauce
- Shredded mozzarella cheese
- Toppings of your choice (such as sliced pepperoni, diced bell peppers, sliced mushrooms, olives, etc.)
- Olive oil
- Italian seasoning or dried oregano (optional)
- Fresh basil leaves, chopped (optional)

Instructions:

1. Preheat Oven: Preheat your oven to 400°F (200°C).
2. Prepare Pita Bread: Place the pita bread rounds on a baking sheet lined with parchment paper or aluminum foil.
3. Add Sauce: Spread a thin layer of pizza sauce or marinara sauce evenly over each pita bread round, leaving a small border around the edges.
4. Add Cheese: Sprinkle shredded mozzarella cheese generously over the sauce on each pita bread.
5. Add Toppings: Add your desired toppings evenly over the cheese. You can customize each pita bread pizza with different toppings if you prefer variety.
6. Drizzle with Olive Oil: Drizzle a little olive oil over the toppings to help them cook and crisp up nicely in the oven.
7. Sprinkle with Seasoning: Optionally, sprinkle some Italian seasoning or dried oregano over the pizzas for added flavor.
8. Bake: Place the baking sheet with the assembled pita bread pizzas in the preheated oven. Bake for 8-10 minutes, or until the cheese is melted and bubbly, and the edges of the pita bread are golden brown and crispy.
9. Serve: Remove from the oven and let the pita bread pizzas cool slightly before slicing. Garnish with chopped fresh basil leaves if desired. Serve warm.

Enjoy your homemade pita bread pizzas as a quick and delicious meal!

Veggie fried rice

Ingredients:

- 2 cups cooked rice (preferably leftover and cooled)
- 2 tablespoons vegetable oil
- 2 cloves garlic, minced
- 1 small onion, finely chopped
- 1 carrot, diced
- 1 bell pepper (any color), diced
- 1 cup frozen peas, thawed
- 2-3 tablespoons soy sauce (adjust to taste)
- 1 tablespoon oyster sauce (optional)
- 2 eggs, lightly beaten
- Salt and pepper, to taste
- Green onions, chopped (for garnish, optional)
- Sesame seeds (for garnish, optional)

Instructions:

1. Prepare Ingredients: Ensure all vegetables are chopped and ready. If you haven't cooked the rice yet, cook it according to package instructions and allow it to cool completely before using it in the recipe.
2. Heat Oil: Heat vegetable oil in a large skillet or wok over medium-high heat.
3. Cook Eggs: Pour the lightly beaten eggs into the skillet. Let them cook undisturbed for a few seconds until they start to set at the edges. Gently scramble the eggs with a spatula until they are fully cooked. Remove them from the skillet and set aside.
4. Stir-fry Vegetables: In the same skillet, add a bit more oil if needed. Add minced garlic and finely chopped onion. Stir-fry for about 1 minute until fragrant.
5. Add diced carrots and bell pepper to the skillet. Stir-fry for 3-4 minutes until the vegetables are tender-crisp.
6. Add Rice: Add the cooked rice to the skillet. Break up any clumps of rice with a spatula and stir-fry for 2-3 minutes to heat through.
7. Season: Drizzle soy sauce and oyster sauce (if using) over the rice and vegetables. Stir well to combine and evenly distribute the sauces. Taste and adjust seasoning with salt and pepper as needed.
8. Add Peas and Eggs: Add thawed peas and cooked eggs back into the skillet. Stir-fry for another minute or until everything is heated through.
9. Serve: Transfer the veggie fried rice to serving plates or bowls. Garnish with chopped green onions and sesame seeds if desired.

Enjoy your homemade veggie fried rice as a delicious and satisfying meal!

BLT sandwich

Ingredients:

- 2-4 slices of bacon (depending on your preference)
- 2 slices of bread (toasted, if desired)
- 1-2 leaves of lettuce (romaine or iceberg work well)
- 1 medium-sized tomato, thinly sliced
- Mayonnaise
- Salt and pepper, to taste

Instructions:

1. Cook the Bacon: In a skillet over medium heat, cook the bacon slices until crispy. Remove from the skillet and drain on paper towels to remove excess grease.
2. Prepare the Bread: If you prefer, toast the bread slices until golden brown.
3. Assemble the Sandwich: Spread mayonnaise on one side of each slice of bread.
4. Layer the Ingredients: On one slice of bread (mayonnaise side up), layer the lettuce leaves, followed by the crispy bacon slices, and then the thinly sliced tomatoes. Season the tomatoes with a sprinkle of salt and pepper, if desired.
5. Close the Sandwich: Place the other slice of bread on top of the tomatoes (mayonnaise side down) to close the sandwich.
6. Cut and Serve: Optionally, cut the sandwich in half diagonally. Serve immediately.

Enjoy your classic BLT sandwich as a quick and satisfying meal!

Baked potatoes with toppings

Ingredients:

- Large baking potatoes (1 per person)
- Olive oil
- Salt
- Toppings of your choice (examples include butter, sour cream, shredded cheese, bacon bits, chopped green onions, salsa, guacamole, etc.)

Instructions:

1. Preheat Oven: Preheat your oven to 400°F (200°C).
2. Prepare Potatoes: Scrub the baking potatoes thoroughly under running water to remove any dirt. Pat them dry with a towel.
3. Poke Holes: Using a fork, poke several holes all around each potato. This allows steam to escape while they bake.
4. Season and Bake: Rub each potato with olive oil and sprinkle generously with salt. Place them directly on the middle rack of your oven.

5. Bake Potatoes: Bake the potatoes for about 45-60 minutes, depending on their size. They are done when you can easily insert a fork into the center with no resistance.
6. Prepare Toppings: While the potatoes are baking, prepare your desired toppings. Shred cheese, chop green onions, crisp bacon bits, etc.
7. Serve: Once the potatoes are done, remove them from the oven and let them cool slightly for a few minutes. Slice each potato lengthwise down the center.
8. Fluff and Add Toppings: Using a fork, gently fluff the inside of each potato to create a fluffy texture. Add your favorite toppings such as butter, sour cream, shredded cheese, bacon bits, chopped green onions, salsa, or guacamole.
9. Enjoy: Serve the loaded baked potatoes immediately while they are still hot.

These loaded baked potatoes are versatile and can be customized to suit various tastes and dietary preferences. They make for a satisfying meal or a substantial side dish.

Macaroni and cheese

Ingredients:

- 2 cups elbow macaroni (or any pasta shape you prefer)
- 2 tablespoons butter
- 2 tablespoons all-purpose flour
- 2 cups milk (preferably whole milk)
- 2 cups shredded cheese (cheddar or a mix of your favorite cheeses)
- Salt and pepper, to taste
- Optional: 1/2 teaspoon mustard powder (for extra flavor)

Instructions:

1. Cook the Pasta: Cook the elbow macaroni in a large pot of salted boiling water according to the package instructions until al dente. Drain and set aside.
2. Make the Cheese Sauce: In the same pot (or a separate saucepan), melt the butter over medium heat. Once melted, add the flour and whisk constantly for about 1-2 minutes to make a roux.
3. Gradually pour in the milk, whisking constantly to prevent lumps from forming. Cook the mixture, stirring frequently, until it thickens and begins to bubble.
4. Add Cheese: Reduce the heat to low. Gradually add the shredded cheese to the milk mixture, stirring until the cheese is melted and the sauce is smooth and creamy. If using mustard powder, add it now and stir to combine. Season with salt and pepper to taste.
5. Combine Pasta and Cheese Sauce: Add the cooked and drained macaroni to the cheese sauce. Stir well until the pasta is evenly coated with the sauce.
6. Serve: Serve the macaroni and cheese hot, optionally garnished with additional shredded cheese or chopped parsley.

Enjoy your homemade macaroni and cheese as a comforting and delicious meal!

Omelette with toast

Ingredients:

- 2-3 large eggs
- Salt and pepper, to taste
- 1 tablespoon butter or cooking oil
- Optional fillings (e.g., diced vegetables, cooked bacon or ham, shredded cheese, herbs like parsley or chives)
- 2 slices of bread (for toasting)

Instructions:

1. Prepare Toast: Start by toasting the bread slices until golden brown. Set them aside.
2. Prepare Omelette: Crack the eggs into a bowl. Season with salt and pepper, then beat the eggs until well combined.
3. Heat Pan: Heat a non-stick skillet over medium heat. Add butter or cooking oil and let it melt or heat up.
4. Cook Omelette: Pour the beaten eggs into the skillet. Let them cook undisturbed for a minute or so until the edges start to set.
5. Add Fillings (if using): Sprinkle any desired fillings (like diced vegetables, cooked meat, or cheese) evenly over the eggs.
6. Fold Omelette: Gently lift one edge of the omelette with a spatula and fold it over towards the center. Repeat with the other edge, creating a neat fold.
7. Finish Cooking: Cook for another minute or so until the omelette is cooked through but still moist on top. You can gently press down on the omelette with the spatula to ensure it's cooked evenly.
8. Serve: Slide the omelette onto a plate and serve with the toasted bread slices.

Enjoy your delicious omelette with toast for a satisfying breakfast or brunch!

Hummus and veggie wraps

Ingredients:

- Large flour tortillas or wraps (whole wheat or regular)
- Hummus (store-bought or homemade)
- Assorted vegetables, thinly sliced or chopped (such as cucumber, bell peppers, carrots, spinach, lettuce, etc.)
- Optional: Sliced avocado, sprouts, olives, or any other favorite veggies
- Optional: Feta cheese, crumbled
- Salt and pepper, to taste

Instructions:

1. Prepare Tortillas: Lay out the tortillas on a clean surface.
2. Spread Hummus: Spread a generous layer of hummus over each tortilla, covering it evenly.
3. Add Vegetables: Layer the assorted vegetables over the hummus-covered tortilla. You can arrange them in a row down the center for easy rolling.
4. Season: Sprinkle salt and pepper over the vegetables to taste.
5. Optional Additions: If using, add sliced avocado, sprouts, olives, or crumbled feta cheese on top of the vegetables.
6. Roll Wraps: Fold in the sides of the tortilla, then roll it up tightly from the bottom to enclose the filling. Press gently to seal.
7. Slice and Serve: Optionally, slice the wraps diagonally in half for easier handling. Serve immediately, or wrap tightly in foil or plastic wrap for later.

These hummus and veggie wraps are perfect for a quick lunch or a light dinner. They are also great for meal prepping ahead of time. Enjoy!

Beef or bean burritos

Ingredients:

- 1 lb ground beef
- 1 small onion, finely chopped
- 2 cloves garlic, minced
- 1 tablespoon chili powder
- 1 teaspoon ground cumin
- 1/2 teaspoon paprika
- Salt and pepper, to taste
- 1 can (15 ounces) refried beans
- 1 cup shredded cheese (cheddar or Mexican blend)
- 4 large flour tortillas
- Optional toppings: Salsa, sour cream, chopped lettuce, diced tomatoes, sliced jalapeños

Instructions:

1. Cook the Beef: In a large skillet, cook the ground beef over medium-high heat until browned and cooked through, breaking it apart with a spatula as it cooks.
2. Add Seasonings: Add the chopped onion, minced garlic, chili powder, ground cumin, paprika, salt, and pepper to the skillet with the cooked beef. Stir well to combine and cook for another 2-3 minutes until the onions are softened and the spices are fragrant.
3. Warm the Tortillas: Heat the flour tortillas in the microwave for a few seconds or in a dry skillet for about 10-15 seconds per side until warm and pliable.
4. Assemble the Burritos: Spread a layer of refried beans down the center of each tortilla. Top with a portion of the seasoned beef mixture and sprinkle with shredded cheese.
5. Roll the Burritos: Fold in the sides of the tortilla, then roll it up tightly from the bottom to enclose the filling. Repeat with the remaining tortillas and filling.
6. Serve: Optionally, heat the burritos in a skillet over medium heat for 1-2 minutes on each side to crisp up the tortilla and melt the cheese. Serve hot with your choice of toppings.

Bean Burritos:

Ingredients:

- 1 can (15 ounces) black beans or pinto beans, drained and rinsed
- 1 teaspoon ground cumin
- 1/2 teaspoon chili powder
- Salt and pepper, to taste
- 1 cup cooked rice (white or brown)
- 1 cup shredded cheese (cheddar or Mexican blend)
- 4 large flour tortillas
- Optional toppings: Salsa, sour cream, chopped lettuce, diced tomatoes, sliced jalapeños

Instructions:

1. Prepare the Beans: In a small saucepan, heat the black beans or pinto beans over medium heat. Add ground cumin, chili powder, salt, and pepper. Mash some of the beans with a fork or potato masher to create a chunky consistency. Cook for 3-5 minutes until heated through.
2. Warm the Tortillas: Heat the flour tortillas in the microwave for a few seconds or in a dry skillet for about 10-15 seconds per side until warm and pliable.
3. Assemble the Burritos: Spread a layer of cooked rice down the center of each tortilla. Top with a portion of the seasoned beans mixture and sprinkle with shredded cheese.
4. Roll the Burritos: Fold in the sides of the tortilla, then roll it up tightly from the bottom to enclose the filling. Repeat with the remaining tortillas and filling.
5. Serve: Optionally, heat the burritos in a skillet over medium heat for 1-2 minutes on each side to warm through and melt the cheese. Serve hot with your choice of toppings.

Enjoy your delicious beef or bean burritos with all the classic toppings for a satisfying meal!

Caesar salad with grilled chicken

Ingredients:

For the Salad:

- 2 boneless, skinless chicken breasts
- Salt and pepper, to taste
- Olive oil
- Romaine lettuce, washed and chopped
- Croutons (store-bought or homemade)
- Shaved or grated Parmesan cheese

For the Caesar Dressing:

- 1/2 cup mayonnaise
- 1/4 cup grated Parmesan cheese
- 2 tablespoons lemon juice (freshly squeezed)
- 1 tablespoon Dijon mustard
- 1 clove garlic, minced
- 1 teaspoon Worcestershire sauce
- Salt and pepper, to taste
- 2-3 tablespoons water (to thin out dressing, if needed)

Instructions:

1. Grill the Chicken:
    - Preheat your grill or grill pan over medium-high heat.
    - Season the chicken breasts with salt, pepper, and a drizzle of olive oil.
    - Grill the chicken for about 5-7 minutes per side, or until cooked through and no longer pink in the center. The internal temperature should reach 165°F (75°C). Once cooked, set aside to rest for a few minutes before slicing.
2. Make the Caesar Dressing:
    - In a bowl, whisk together mayonnaise, grated Parmesan cheese, lemon juice, Dijon mustard, minced garlic, Worcestershire sauce, salt, and pepper until smooth.
    - If the dressing is too thick, add 2-3 tablespoons of water gradually until you reach your desired consistency. Taste and adjust seasoning as needed.
3. Assemble the Salad:
    - In a large salad bowl, toss the chopped romaine lettuce with enough Caesar dressing to coat the leaves evenly. Add more dressing as needed.
    - Add croutons and shaved or grated Parmesan cheese to the salad bowl and toss again gently to combine.
4. Slice the Chicken:
    - Slice the grilled chicken breasts into thin slices or cubes.

5. Serve:
    - Arrange the dressed Caesar salad on plates or in bowls.
    - Top each portion with slices of grilled chicken.
6. Optional Garnish:
    - Garnish with additional shaved or grated Parmesan cheese, freshly ground black pepper, and extra croutons if desired.

Enjoy your delicious Caesar salad with grilled chicken as a main course or hearty lunch!

Tomato soup with grilled cheese

Ingredients:

- 2 tablespoons olive oil
- 1 onion, chopped
- 2 cloves garlic, minced
- 1 can (28 ounces) whole peeled tomatoes
- 1 can (14 ounces) crushed tomatoes
- 2 cups vegetable or chicken broth
- 1 teaspoon dried basil
- 1 teaspoon dried oregano
- Salt and pepper, to taste
- 1/2 cup heavy cream or half-and-half (optional, for a creamy soup)

Instructions:

1. Sauté Onion and Garlic: Heat olive oil in a large pot over medium heat. Add chopped onion and sauté until softened, about 5 minutes. Add minced garlic and cook for another 1-2 minutes until fragrant.
2. Add Tomatoes and Broth: Pour in the whole peeled tomatoes (crush them with your hands or a spoon as you add them to the pot) and crushed tomatoes. Stir in the vegetable or chicken broth.
3. Season: Add dried basil, dried oregano, salt, and pepper to the pot. Stir well to combine.
4. Simmer: Bring the soup to a boil, then reduce the heat to low. Let it simmer uncovered for about 20-25 minutes, stirring occasionally, to allow the flavors to meld and the soup to thicken slightly.
5. Blend (Optional): For a smoother soup, use an immersion blender directly in the pot to blend until smooth. Alternatively, carefully transfer the soup in batches to a blender and blend until smooth, then return it to the pot.
6. Add Cream (Optional): Stir in the heavy cream or half-and-half, if using, to add richness and creaminess to the soup. Adjust seasoning with more salt and pepper if needed.
7. Serve: Ladle the tomato soup into bowls and serve hot.

Grilled Cheese Sandwich:

Ingredients:

- 4 slices of bread (any type you prefer)
- Butter, softened
- 4 slices of cheese (cheddar, American, Swiss, or your favorite melting cheese)

Instructions:

1. Butter the Bread: Spread softened butter on one side of each slice of bread.

2. Assemble the Sandwiches: Place the bread slices butter-side down on a clean surface. Place a slice of cheese on each slice of bread.
3. Cook the Sandwiches: Heat a non-stick skillet or griddle over medium heat. Carefully place the assembled sandwiches in the skillet, butter-side down.
4. Grill: Cook for 2-4 minutes on each side, or until the bread is golden brown and crispy, and the cheese inside is melted.
5. Serve: Remove the grilled cheese sandwiches from the skillet and let them cool for a minute before slicing them diagonally (optional) and serving alongside the tomato soup.

Enjoy this comforting meal of tomato soup with grilled cheese sandwiches, perfect for a cozy lunch or dinner!

Stuffed bell peppers

Ingredients:

- 4 large bell peppers (any color)
- 1 lb ground beef or turkey
- 1 cup cooked rice (white or brown)
- 1 small onion, finely chopped
- 2 cloves garlic, minced
- 1 can (14.5 ounces) diced tomatoes, drained
- 1 cup shredded cheese (cheddar, mozzarella, or a blend)
- 1 teaspoon dried oregano
- 1 teaspoon dried basil
- Salt and pepper, to taste
- Optional: 1/2 cup tomato sauce or marinara sauce
- Optional toppings: Chopped fresh parsley, grated Parmesan cheese

Instructions:

1. Preheat Oven: Preheat your oven to 375°F (190°C).
2. Prepare Bell Peppers: Cut the tops off the bell peppers and remove the seeds and membranes from inside. Rinse the peppers under cold water.
3. Cook the Filling: In a large skillet, cook the ground beef or turkey over medium-high heat until browned and cooked through, breaking it apart with a spatula as it cooks. Drain any excess fat.
4. Add Aromatics: Add the chopped onion and minced garlic to the skillet with the cooked meat. Cook for 2-3 minutes until the onion is softened and translucent.
5. Combine Ingredients: Stir in the cooked rice, drained diced tomatoes, dried oregano, dried basil, salt, and pepper. If using tomato sauce or marinara sauce, add it now and mix well. Cook for another 2-3 minutes until heated through.
6. Stuff the Peppers: Arrange the bell peppers upright in a baking dish. Spoon the filling mixture evenly into each pepper until they are full.
7. Bake: Cover the baking dish with foil and bake in the preheated oven for 30-35 minutes, or until the peppers are tender.
8. Add Cheese: Remove the foil and sprinkle shredded cheese over the tops of each stuffed pepper. Return the peppers to the oven and bake for an additional 5-10 minutes, or until the cheese is melted and bubbly.
9. Serve: Remove the stuffed bell peppers from the oven and let them cool for a few minutes. Garnish with chopped fresh parsley and grated Parmesan cheese if desired. Serve hot.

Enjoy your hearty and flavorful stuffed bell peppers as a satisfying meal!

Chicken fajitas

Ingredients:

- 1 lb chicken breasts or thighs, thinly sliced
- 2 tablespoons olive oil
- 1 onion, thinly sliced
- 1 bell pepper (any color), thinly sliced
- 1-2 cloves garlic, minced
- 1 tablespoon chili powder
- 1 teaspoon ground cumin
- 1/2 teaspoon paprika
- Salt and pepper, to taste
- Juice of 1 lime
- 8 small flour tortillas (6-inch size)
- Optional toppings: Sliced avocado or guacamole, sour cream, salsa, shredded cheese, chopped cilantro, lime wedges

Instructions:

1. Marinate the Chicken: In a bowl, combine the thinly sliced chicken with olive oil, minced garlic, chili powder, ground cumin, paprika, salt, pepper, and lime juice. Mix well to coat the chicken evenly. Let it marinate for at least 15-20 minutes.
2. Cook the Chicken and Vegetables: Heat a large skillet or grill pan over medium-high heat. Add a drizzle of olive oil if needed. Add the marinated chicken slices to the skillet in a single layer. Cook for 4-5 minutes, stirring occasionally, until the chicken is cooked through and slightly charred. Remove the chicken from the skillet and set aside.
3. In the same skillet, add a bit more olive oil if needed. Add sliced onions and bell peppers. Cook for 5-6 minutes, stirring occasionally, until the vegetables are tender-crisp and slightly charred.
4. Combine Chicken and Vegetables: Return the cooked chicken to the skillet with the vegetables. Stir everything together and cook for another 1-2 minutes to heat through.
5. Warm Tortillas: While the chicken and vegetables are cooking, heat the flour tortillas. You can warm them directly over a gas flame (using tongs to flip them), in a dry skillet, or wrapped in foil in a low oven until warmed through and pliable.
6. Assemble Fajitas: Spoon the chicken and vegetable mixture onto warmed tortillas. Add your desired toppings such as sliced avocado or guacamole, sour cream, salsa, shredded cheese, and chopped cilantro.
7. Serve: Serve the chicken fajitas immediately with lime wedges on the side for squeezing over the top.

Enjoy your homemade chicken fajitas with all the delicious toppings for a flavorful and satisfying meal!

Greek yogurt with granola and fruit

Ingredients:

- Greek yogurt (plain or flavored, depending on your preference)
- Granola (store-bought or homemade)
- Fresh fruits (such as berries, sliced bananas, diced mango, or any seasonal fruit of your choice)
- Optional: Honey or maple syrup for drizzling

Instructions:

1. Prepare the Yogurt: Spoon Greek yogurt into a bowl or serving dish. Use as much yogurt as you prefer, depending on your appetite.
2. Add Granola: Sprinkle granola over the yogurt. Use enough to add crunch and texture to your dish.
3. Add Fresh Fruit: Arrange fresh fruits over the yogurt and granola. You can mix and match fruits or arrange them in sections for a visually appealing presentation.
4. Optional Drizzle: If you prefer extra sweetness, drizzle honey or maple syrup over the yogurt and fruits.
5. Serve: Enjoy your Greek yogurt with granola and fruit immediately as a satisfying and wholesome breakfast or snack.

Variations:

- Nutty Crunch: Add chopped nuts such as almonds, walnuts, or pecans to the granola for extra crunch and protein.
- Creamy Texture: For a creamier texture, mix a bit of milk or almond milk into the yogurt before adding granola and fruit.
- Flavor Boost: Sprinkle cinnamon, nutmeg, or a dash of vanilla extract over the yogurt for added flavor.

This versatile dish can be customized with your favorite fruits and toppings, making it a delicious and nutritious choice any time of day.

Pancakes with syrup and fruit

Ingredients:

- 1 cup all-purpose flour
- 2 tablespoons granulated sugar
- 1 teaspoon baking powder
- 1/2 teaspoon baking soda
- 1/4 teaspoon salt
- 3/4 cup milk
- 1 large egg
- 2 tablespoons unsalted butter, melted
- 1 teaspoon vanilla extract (optional)
- Butter or oil for cooking
- Maple syrup, for serving
- Fresh fruits (such as berries, sliced bananas, or diced mango), for topping

Instructions:

1. Prepare Dry Ingredients: In a mixing bowl, whisk together the flour, sugar, baking powder, baking soda, and salt.
2. Prepare Wet Ingredients: In another bowl, whisk together the milk, egg, melted butter, and vanilla extract (if using).
3. Combine Batter: Pour the wet ingredients into the dry ingredients. Stir gently with a spoon or whisk until just combined. It's okay if there are a few lumps in the batter.
4. Heat Griddle or Pan: Heat a non-stick skillet or griddle over medium heat. Add a small amount of butter or oil and spread it evenly across the surface.
5. Cook Pancakes: Pour about 1/4 cup of batter onto the skillet for each pancake. Cook until bubbles form on the surface of the pancake and the edges look set, about 2-3 minutes.
6. Flip and Cook: Carefully flip the pancakes with a spatula and cook for another 1-2 minutes, or until golden brown and cooked through.
7. Serve: Transfer the pancakes to a plate. Top with maple syrup and arrange fresh fruits on top. Optionally, add a small pat of butter on top of the warm pancakes before serving.
8. Enjoy: Serve the pancakes warm and enjoy with your favorite combination of syrup and fresh fruits.

Tips:

- Keep pancakes warm: Place cooked pancakes on a baking sheet in a warm oven (about 200°F or 90°C) while you finish cooking the remaining pancakes.
- Customize toppings: Besides fruits, you can also add whipped cream, yogurt, nuts, or chocolate chips to your pancakes for extra flavor and texture.

This recipe yields fluffy pancakes that are perfect for stacking and enjoying with syrup and fresh fruit for a delicious breakfast treat!

Caprese salad

Ingredients:

- Fresh ripe tomatoes, sliced (about 2-3 medium tomatoes)
- Fresh mozzarella cheese, sliced (about 8 ounces)
- Fresh basil leaves
- Extra virgin olive oil
- Balsamic vinegar (optional)
- Salt and pepper, to taste

Instructions:

1. Prepare Ingredients: Wash and slice the tomatoes and fresh mozzarella cheese into rounds, approximately 1/4-inch thick.
2. Assemble Salad: Arrange the tomato slices and mozzarella slices alternately on a serving platter or individual plates, overlapping slightly.
3. Add Basil Leaves: Tuck fresh basil leaves between the tomato and mozzarella slices. You can use whole leaves or chiffonade (thinly sliced).
4. Season: Drizzle extra virgin olive oil over the salad. Optionally, drizzle balsamic vinegar for added flavor (traditional balsamic or a balsamic reduction works well). Season with salt and pepper to taste.
5. Serve: Serve the Caprese salad immediately as an appetizer or side dish. It can also be served with crusty bread to soak up the flavorful juices.

Variations:

- Caprese Skewers: Thread cherry tomatoes, mini mozzarella balls (bocconcini), and basil leaves onto skewers for a fun and portable version of Caprese salad.
- Caprese Salad Platter: Arrange the ingredients in a platter format for a larger serving, drizzling the olive oil and balsamic vinegar over the top.
- Caprese Salad Wraps: Wrap the ingredients in large lettuce leaves or flatbreads for a handheld version of Caprese salad.

Caprese salad is best enjoyed when the ingredients are fresh and at room temperature. It's a perfect dish for showcasing the flavors of summer and makes a beautiful addition to any meal or gathering.

Avocado toast with poached egg

Ingredients:

- 1 ripe avocado
- 2 slices of bread (whole grain or your preferred type)
- 2 eggs
- Salt and pepper, to taste
- Optional toppings: Red pepper flakes, paprika, sesame seeds, chopped herbs (such as cilantro or parsley)

Instructions:

1. Prepare Avocado: Cut the ripe avocado in half, remove the pit, and scoop the flesh into a bowl. Mash the avocado with a fork until smooth or leave it slightly chunky if desired. Season with salt and pepper to taste.
2. Toast Bread: Toast the slices of bread until golden brown and crispy.
3. Poach Eggs: While the bread is toasting, poach the eggs. Here's a simple method for poaching eggs:
    - Fill a medium-sized saucepan with water, about 2-3 inches deep. Bring the water to a gentle simmer over medium heat.
    - Crack each egg into a small bowl or ramekin.
    - Using a spoon, create a gentle whirlpool in the simmering water.
    - Carefully slide each egg into the center of the whirlpool. Cook for about 3-4 minutes, or until the whites are set but the yolks are still soft.
    - Remove the poached eggs with a slotted spoon and drain on a paper towel.
4. Assemble Avocado Toast: Spread a generous amount of mashed avocado onto each slice of toasted bread.
5. Top with Poached Egg: Carefully place a poached egg on top of each slice of avocado toast.
6. Season and Serve: Season the poached eggs with a sprinkle of salt, pepper, and any optional toppings you prefer, such as red pepper flakes, paprika, sesame seeds, or chopped herbs.
7. Enjoy: Serve the avocado toast with poached egg immediately while the eggs are still warm and the toast is crispy.

Avocado toast with poached egg is not only delicious but also packed with healthy fats, protein, and fiber, making it a satisfying and nutritious breakfast option.

Quinoa salad with vegetables

Ingredients:

- 1 cup quinoa (any color, such as white, red, or mixed)
- 2 cups water or vegetable broth
- 1 cucumber, diced
- 1 bell pepper (any color), diced
- 1 cup cherry tomatoes, halved
- 1/2 red onion, finely chopped
- 1/4 cup fresh parsley or cilantro, chopped
- Juice of 1-2 lemons (about 1/4 cup)
- 3 tablespoons extra virgin olive oil
- Salt and pepper, to taste
- Optional: Crumbled feta cheese, sliced olives, chopped avocado

Instructions:

1. Cook Quinoa: Rinse the quinoa under cold water using a fine mesh sieve. In a medium saucepan, combine quinoa and water or vegetable broth. Bring to a boil over medium-high heat. Reduce heat to low, cover, and simmer for 15-20 minutes, or until the quinoa is cooked and all the liquid is absorbed. Remove from heat and let it cool slightly.
2. Prepare Vegetables: While the quinoa is cooking, prepare the vegetables. Dice the cucumber, bell pepper, cherry tomatoes, and finely chop the red onion. Chop the parsley or cilantro.
3. Assemble Salad: In a large bowl, combine the cooked quinoa and prepared vegetables. Add chopped parsley or cilantro.
4. Make Dressing: In a small bowl, whisk together lemon juice, extra virgin olive oil, salt, and pepper.
5. Combine and Toss: Pour the dressing over the quinoa and vegetables. Toss gently to combine, ensuring the salad is evenly coated with the dressing.
6. Add Optional Ingredients: If desired, add crumbled feta cheese, sliced olives, or chopped avocado to the salad and gently toss again.
7. Chill and Serve: Cover the quinoa salad and refrigerate for at least 30 minutes to allow the flavors to meld. Serve chilled or at room temperature.
8. Enjoy: Enjoy the quinoa salad with vegetables as a refreshing and nutritious meal or side dish.

This quinoa salad is versatile, packed with nutrients, and can be customized with your favorite vegetables and toppings. It's perfect for meal prep, picnics, or as a side dish for barbecues and gatherings.

Sloppy Joes

Ingredients:

- 1 lb ground beef or ground turkey
- 1 small onion, finely chopped
- 1/2 green bell pepper, finely chopped
- 2 cloves garlic, minced
- 1 cup tomato sauce
- 1/2 cup ketchup
- 1 tablespoon brown sugar
- 1 tablespoon Worcestershire sauce
- 1 teaspoon mustard (yellow or Dijon)
- 1/2 teaspoon chili powder (adjust to taste)
- Salt and pepper, to taste
- Hamburger buns, for serving

Instructions:

1. Cook the Meat: In a large skillet or frying pan, cook the ground beef or turkey over medium-high heat until browned and cooked through, breaking it apart with a spoon as it cooks. Drain any excess fat if needed.
2. Sauté Vegetables: Add chopped onion and green bell pepper to the skillet with the cooked meat. Cook for 3-4 minutes until the vegetables are softened.
3. Add Seasonings: Stir in minced garlic, tomato sauce, ketchup, brown sugar, Worcestershire sauce, mustard, chili powder, salt, and pepper. Mix well to combine.
4. Simmer: Reduce the heat to low and let the mixture simmer for 10-15 minutes, stirring occasionally, to allow the flavors to meld and the sauce to thicken slightly. Taste and adjust seasoning if needed.
5. Toast Hamburger Buns: While the Sloppy Joe mixture is simmering, toast the hamburger buns under the broiler or in a toaster until lightly golden.
6. Assemble and Serve: Spoon a generous amount of the Sloppy Joe mixture onto the bottom half of each toasted hamburger bun. Top with the other half of the bun.
7. Enjoy: Serve Sloppy Joes immediately while warm, accompanied by your favorite sides such as coleslaw, potato chips, or pickles.

Sloppy Joes are versatile and can be customized to suit your taste preferences. You can adjust the seasoning, add more vegetables, or even swap ground beef with ground turkey for a lighter version. It's a hearty and satisfying dish that's perfect for family dinners or casual gatherings.

Spinach and cheese stuffed pasta shells

Ingredients:

- 1 box (12 ounces) jumbo pasta shells
- 1 tablespoon olive oil
- 1 small onion, finely chopped
- 2 cloves garlic, minced
- 5 ounces fresh spinach, chopped (about 5 cups packed)
- 15 ounces ricotta cheese
- 1 cup shredded mozzarella cheese, divided
- 1/2 cup grated Parmesan cheese, divided
- 1 egg
- 1 teaspoon dried Italian herbs (or use a mixture of dried basil, oregano, and thyme)
- Salt and pepper, to taste
- 2 cups marinara sauce

Instructions:

1. Cook Pasta Shells: Cook the jumbo pasta shells according to package instructions until al dente. Drain and set aside to cool.
2. Prepare Filling: In a large skillet, heat olive oil over medium heat. Add chopped onion and garlic, sauté for 3-4 minutes until softened. Add chopped spinach and cook until wilted, about 2-3 minutes. Remove from heat and let it cool slightly.
3. Combine Ingredients: In a large bowl, combine ricotta cheese, 3/4 cup shredded mozzarella cheese, 1/4 cup grated Parmesan cheese, egg, dried Italian herbs, salt, and pepper. Add the cooked spinach mixture and stir until well combined.
4. Stuff Pasta Shells: Preheat oven to 375°F (190°C). Spread 1 cup marinara sauce evenly over the bottom of a 9x13-inch baking dish. Spoon the spinach and cheese mixture into each cooked pasta shell, filling them generously. Arrange the stuffed shells in a single layer in the baking dish.
5. Bake: Spoon the remaining marinara sauce over the stuffed shells. Sprinkle the remaining 1/4 cup shredded mozzarella cheese and 1/4 cup grated Parmesan cheese over the top.
6. Cover and Bake: Cover the baking dish with aluminum foil and bake in the preheated oven for 25-30 minutes, or until the cheese is melted and bubbly.
7. Serve: Remove from the oven and let it cool for a few minutes before serving. Optionally, garnish with chopped fresh basil or parsley before serving.

Enjoy these spinach and cheese stuffed pasta shells as a satisfying main dish, accompanied by a side salad or garlic bread. They're perfect for a cozy family dinner or special occasion meal.

Teriyaki chicken bowl with rice

Ingredients:

For Teriyaki Chicken:

- 1 lb boneless, skinless chicken breasts or thighs, cut into bite-sized pieces
- 1/2 cup teriyaki sauce (store-bought or homemade)
- 2 tablespoons soy sauce
- 2 tablespoons honey or brown sugar
- 2 cloves garlic, minced
- 1 teaspoon grated fresh ginger (optional)
- 1 tablespoon vegetable oil
- Salt and pepper, to taste
- Sesame seeds, for garnish (optional)
- Sliced green onions, for garnish (optional)

For Rice and Bowl:

- 2 cups cooked white or brown rice
- Steamed or stir-fried vegetables (such as broccoli, carrots, bell peppers, snap peas, etc.)
- Optional toppings: Sliced avocado, shredded cabbage, sliced cucumber, edamame, sesame seeds

Instructions:

1. Marinate Chicken: In a bowl, combine teriyaki sauce, soy sauce, honey or brown sugar, minced garlic, and grated ginger (if using). Add the chicken pieces and stir to coat. Let it marinate for at least 15-20 minutes, or refrigerate for up to 1 hour for more flavor.
2. Cook Chicken: Heat vegetable oil in a large skillet or wok over medium-high heat. Add the marinated chicken pieces in a single layer (reserve the marinade). Cook for 5-6 minutes, stirring occasionally, until the chicken is cooked through and nicely caramelized. Remove chicken from the skillet and set aside.
3. Make Teriyaki Sauce: Pour the reserved marinade into the skillet. Bring it to a boil, then reduce heat to medium-low and simmer for 3-4 minutes until slightly thickened. Return the cooked chicken to the skillet and toss to coat evenly with the teriyaki sauce. Remove from heat.
4. Assemble Bowls: Divide cooked rice among serving bowls. Top each bowl with teriyaki chicken and steamed or stir-fried vegetables of your choice.
5. Garnish and Serve: Garnish with sesame seeds and sliced green onions, if desired. Add any optional toppings such as sliced avocado, shredded cabbage, sliced cucumber, or edamame.
6. Enjoy: Serve teriyaki chicken bowls immediately while warm. Mix everything together before eating to enjoy all the flavors.

This teriyaki chicken bowl with rice is a complete and satisfying meal that combines savory teriyaki chicken with nutritious vegetables and rice. It's customizable with your favorite vegetables and toppings, making it perfect for a quick and delicious dinner or lunch option.

Chicken Caesar wraps

Ingredients:

- 2 cups cooked chicken breast, shredded or diced
- 1/2 cup Caesar salad dressing (store-bought or homemade)
- 1/4 cup grated Parmesan cheese
- 1 cup shredded romaine lettuce
- 1/2 cup cherry tomatoes, halved
- 1/4 cup croutons
- 4 large flour tortillas (burrito size)
- Salt and pepper, to taste

Instructions:

1. Prepare Chicken: Cook chicken breast if not already cooked. You can boil, bake, or grill the chicken until fully cooked, then shred or dice it into bite-sized pieces.
2. Mix Chicken with Dressing: In a large bowl, combine the cooked chicken with Caesar salad dressing. Mix well to coat the chicken evenly. Add grated Parmesan cheese and season with salt and pepper to taste.
3. Assemble Wraps: Lay out the flour tortillas on a clean surface. Place shredded romaine lettuce evenly down the center of each tortilla.
4. Add Chicken Mixture: Spoon the Caesar chicken mixture evenly on top of the lettuce on each tortilla.
5. Add Toppings: Sprinkle halved cherry tomatoes and croutons over the chicken mixture.
6. Wrap: Fold in the sides of each tortilla, then roll up tightly from the bottom to enclose the filling.
7. Serve: Cut the wraps in half diagonally if desired, and serve immediately.

Optional: You can add additional toppings or ingredients to customize your chicken Caesar wraps, such as crispy bacon bits, avocado slices, or extra Parmesan cheese.

These chicken Caesar wraps are perfect for a quick lunch or dinner, whether at home or packed for on-the-go. They are flavorful, satisfying, and packed with protein and veggies, making them a balanced meal option. Enjoy!

Veggie chili

Ingredients:

- 1 tablespoon olive oil
- 1 onion, diced
- 3 cloves garlic, minced
- 1 bell pepper (any color), diced
- 2 carrots, diced
- 2 celery stalks, diced
- 1 zucchini, diced
- 1 yellow squash, diced
- 1 can (15 ounces) kidney beans, drained and rinsed
- 1 can (15 ounces) black beans, drained and rinsed
- 1 can (15 ounces) diced tomatoes
- 1 cup corn kernels (fresh or frozen)
- 1 tablespoon chili powder
- 1 teaspoon ground cumin
- 1 teaspoon smoked paprika
- 1/2 teaspoon dried oregano
- 1/2 teaspoon ground coriander
- Salt and pepper, to taste
- 2 cups vegetable broth or water
- Optional toppings: Shredded cheese, sour cream, chopped cilantro, diced avocado, lime wedges

Instructions:

1. Sauté Vegetables: Heat olive oil in a large pot or Dutch oven over medium heat. Add diced onion and garlic, sauté for 3-4 minutes until softened and fragrant.
2. Add Vegetables: Add diced bell pepper, carrots, celery, zucchini, and yellow squash to the pot. Cook for 5-6 minutes, stirring occasionally, until vegetables are slightly tender.
3. Add Beans and Tomatoes: Stir in kidney beans, black beans, diced tomatoes (with juices), and corn kernels. Mix well to combine.
4. Season: Add chili powder, ground cumin, smoked paprika, dried oregano, ground coriander, salt, and pepper to taste. Stir to coat the vegetables and beans with the spices.
5. Simmer: Pour vegetable broth or water into the pot. Bring the chili to a simmer over medium-high heat, then reduce heat to low. Cover and let it simmer for 20-30 minutes, stirring occasionally, until flavors are well blended and vegetables are tender.
6. Adjust Seasoning: Taste and adjust seasoning if needed, adding more salt, pepper, or chili powder according to your preference.
7. Serve: Ladle the veggie chili into bowls. Serve hot, topped with shredded cheese, a dollop of sour cream, chopped cilantro, diced avocado, and a squeeze of lime juice if desired.

8. Enjoy: Enjoy your flavorful and nutritious veggie chili as a satisfying meal. It pairs well with crusty bread, cornbread, or over cooked rice.

This veggie chili recipe is versatile and can be adapted based on the vegetables you have on hand or your personal preferences. It's a great way to enjoy a comforting and healthy dish packed with plant-based proteins and fiber.

Pesto pasta with cherry tomatoes

Ingredients:

- 12 ounces pasta of your choice (such as spaghetti, penne, or fusilli)
- 1/2 cup basil pesto (store-bought or homemade)
- 1 pint cherry tomatoes, halved
- 1/4 cup grated Parmesan cheese
- Salt and pepper, to taste
- Optional: Crushed red pepper flakes, pine nuts, fresh basil leaves for garnish

Instructions:

1. Cook Pasta: Cook the pasta according to package instructions in a large pot of salted boiling water until al dente. Drain the pasta, reserving about 1/2 cup of pasta water.
2. Combine with Pesto: In a large bowl, toss the cooked pasta with basil pesto until well coated. If the pesto is too thick, add a tablespoon or two of reserved pasta water to loosen it up.
3. Add Cherry Tomatoes: Gently fold in halved cherry tomatoes into the pasta and pesto mixture. The heat from the pasta will slightly warm the tomatoes.
4. Season: Season with salt and pepper to taste. Be mindful of the salt content in both the pesto and Parmesan cheese.
5. Serve: Transfer the pesto pasta to serving plates or a large serving bowl. Sprinkle grated Parmesan cheese over the top. Optionally, garnish with crushed red pepper flakes, pine nuts, or fresh basil leaves for extra flavor and presentation.
6. Enjoy: Serve the pesto pasta with cherry tomatoes immediately while warm. It's delicious as a main dish or as a side with grilled chicken or seafood.

Tips:

- Homemade Pesto: If making pesto from scratch, blend fresh basil leaves, garlic, Parmesan cheese, pine nuts (or almonds), and olive oil in a food processor until smooth. Adjust seasoning to taste.
- Variations: You can add other ingredients such as cooked chicken, shrimp, or grilled vegetables to the pasta for added protein and texture.

This pesto pasta with cherry tomatoes is quick to prepare and bursting with fresh flavors. It's perfect for a weeknight dinner or a casual gathering with friends and family. Enjoy!

Tacos with ground beef or beans

Ground Beef Tacos

Ingredients:

- 1 lb ground beef
- 1 small onion, finely chopped
- 2 cloves garlic, minced
- 1 tablespoon chili powder
- 1 teaspoon ground cumin
- 1/2 teaspoon paprika
- 1/4 teaspoon cayenne pepper (optional, for heat)
- Salt and pepper, to taste
- 1/2 cup tomato sauce or diced tomatoes
- 1/2 cup beef broth or water
- 8-10 small tortillas (corn or flour)
- Toppings: Shredded lettuce, diced tomatoes, shredded cheese, salsa, sour cream, chopped cilantro, lime wedges

Instructions:

1. Cook Ground Beef: In a large skillet or frying pan, cook the ground beef over medium-high heat until browned and cooked through, breaking it apart with a spoon as it cooks. Drain any excess fat if needed.
2. Add Aromatics and Spices: Add chopped onion and minced garlic to the skillet with the cooked beef. Cook for 2-3 minutes until onion is softened and garlic is fragrant.
3. Season: Stir in chili powder, ground cumin, paprika, cayenne pepper (if using), salt, and pepper. Mix well to coat the beef and vegetables with the spices.
4. Add Tomato Sauce and Broth: Pour tomato sauce (or diced tomatoes) and beef broth (or water) into the skillet. Bring to a simmer and cook for 5-7 minutes, stirring occasionally, until the sauce thickens slightly and flavors meld. Adjust seasoning to taste.
5. Warm Tortillas: Meanwhile, heat the tortillas in a dry skillet or microwave until warm and pliable.
6. Assemble Tacos: Spoon the ground beef mixture onto the warmed tortillas. Top with shredded lettuce, diced tomatoes, shredded cheese, salsa, sour cream, chopped cilantro, and a squeeze of lime juice.
7. Serve: Serve ground beef tacos immediately, with additional toppings on the side.

Bean Tacos

Ingredients:

- 1 can (15 ounces) black beans or pinto beans, drained and rinsed
- 1 tablespoon olive oil

- 1 small onion, finely chopped
- 2 cloves garlic, minced
- 1 teaspoon ground cumin
- 1/2 teaspoon chili powder
- Salt and pepper, to taste
- 1/4 cup water or vegetable broth
- 8-10 small tortillas (corn or flour)
- Toppings: Shredded lettuce, diced tomatoes, shredded cheese, salsa, sour cream, chopped cilantro, lime wedges

Instructions:

1. Cook Beans: In a large skillet or frying pan, heat olive oil over medium heat. Add chopped onion and minced garlic, sauté for 3-4 minutes until softened.
2. Add Spices: Stir in ground cumin, chili powder, salt, and pepper. Cook for another minute until fragrant.
3. Add Beans and Liquid: Add black beans (or pinto beans) to the skillet. Pour in water (or vegetable broth) and stir to combine. Bring to a simmer and cook for 5-7 minutes, stirring occasionally, until beans are heated through and flavors meld. Mash some of the beans with the back of a spoon for a thicker consistency if desired.
4. Warm Tortillas: Heat the tortillas in a dry skillet or microwave until warm and pliable.
5. Assemble Tacos: Spoon the bean mixture onto the warmed tortillas. Top with shredded lettuce, diced tomatoes, shredded cheese, salsa, sour cream, chopped cilantro, and a squeeze of lime juice.
6. Serve: Serve bean tacos immediately, with additional toppings on the side.

Both ground beef tacos and bean tacos are customizable to your taste preferences and make for a delicious and satisfying meal. Enjoy these flavorful tacos with your favorite toppings for a tasty and versatile dinner option!

Baked chicken drumsticks

Ingredients:

- 8 chicken drumsticks
- 2 tablespoons olive oil
- 2 cloves garlic, minced
- 1 teaspoon paprika
- 1 teaspoon dried thyme (or use any herbs of your choice, such as rosemary or oregano)
- 1/2 teaspoon onion powder
- 1/2 teaspoon salt, or to taste
- 1/4 teaspoon black pepper, or to taste
- Optional: Lemon wedges, chopped fresh herbs (parsley or thyme) for garnish

Instructions:

1. Preheat Oven: Preheat your oven to 425°F (220°C). Line a baking sheet with parchment paper or foil for easier cleanup.
2. Prepare Chicken: Pat the chicken drumsticks dry with paper towels. This helps the skin to crisp up better.
3. Season Chicken: In a small bowl, mix together olive oil, minced garlic, paprika, dried thyme (or other herbs), onion powder, salt, and black pepper.
4. Coat Chicken: Place the chicken drumsticks in a large bowl or a resealable plastic bag. Pour the olive oil mixture over the drumsticks and toss until evenly coated.
5. Arrange on Baking Sheet: Arrange the chicken drumsticks in a single layer on the prepared baking sheet.
6. Bake: Bake in the preheated oven for 30-35 minutes, or until the chicken is golden brown and cooked through, with an internal temperature of 165°F (74°C).
7. Rest and Serve: Remove from the oven and let the chicken drumsticks rest for a few minutes before serving. This helps to redistribute the juices.
8. Garnish and Enjoy: Garnish with lemon wedges and chopped fresh herbs if desired. Serve hot as a main dish with your favorite sides, such as roasted vegetables, mashed potatoes, or a crisp salad.

Baked chicken drumsticks are versatile and can be enjoyed for a casual family dinner or served at gatherings. They're crispy on the outside and tender on the inside, making them a favorite among both kids and adults. Adjust the seasoning according to your taste preferences and enjoy this simple yet delicious dish!

Pad Thai noodles

Ingredients:

- 8 ounces rice noodles (pad Thai noodles)
- 2 tablespoons vegetable oil
- 1 shallot, thinly sliced
- 2 cloves garlic, minced
- 1/2 cup tofu, cubed (optional)
- 1/2 lb shrimp, peeled and deveined (or substitute with chicken, beef, or more tofu)
- 2 eggs, lightly beaten
- 1 cup bean sprouts
- 1/2 cup chopped green onions
- 1/4 cup chopped roasted peanuts
- Lime wedges, for serving

For the Sauce:

- 3 tablespoons tamarind paste
- 3 tablespoons fish sauce (or soy sauce for vegetarian version)
- 2 tablespoons brown sugar (adjust to taste)
- 1 tablespoon rice vinegar
- 1 teaspoon sriracha sauce (optional, for heat)

Instructions:

1. Prepare Rice Noodles: Cook the rice noodles according to package instructions until al dente. Drain and set aside.
2. Make Sauce: In a small bowl, whisk together tamarind paste, fish sauce (or soy sauce), brown sugar, rice vinegar, and sriracha sauce (if using). Adjust the sweetness and tanginess to your taste by adding more sugar or vinegar if needed.
3. Stir-Fry: Heat vegetable oil in a large wok or skillet over medium-high heat. Add sliced shallot and minced garlic, stir-fry for 1-2 minutes until fragrant.
4. Add Protein: Push the shallot and garlic to the side of the wok. Add cubed tofu (if using) and cook until lightly browned. Push tofu to the side and add shrimp (or other protein). Cook until shrimp are pink and cooked through.
5. Scramble Eggs: Push the tofu and shrimp to the side and pour beaten eggs into the empty space. Let the eggs cook for a few seconds until they begin to set. Scramble the eggs with a spatula until fully cooked and mixed with the tofu and shrimp.
6. Combine with Noodles: Add cooked rice noodles to the wok or skillet. Pour the prepared sauce over the noodles. Toss everything together using tongs or chopsticks until well combined and heated through.
7. Add Vegetables and Toppings: Add bean sprouts and chopped green onions to the noodles. Toss briefly to mix. Remove from heat.

8. Serve: Divide Pad Thai noodles among serving plates. Garnish with chopped roasted peanuts and serve with lime wedges on the side.
9. Enjoy: Serve Pad Thai noodles hot, squeezing lime juice over each serving just before eating.

Pad Thai noodles are best enjoyed fresh and hot, with a balance of flavors from sweet, tangy, savory, and a hint of heat. Customize the toppings and protein according to your preference for a delicious homemade Thai-inspired dish!

Minestrone soup

Ingredients:

- 2 tablespoons olive oil
- 1 onion, diced
- 2 cloves garlic, minced
- 2 carrots, diced
- 2 celery stalks, diced
- 1 zucchini, diced
- 1 yellow squash, diced
- 1 potato, peeled and diced
- 1 can (15 ounces) diced tomatoes
- 4 cups vegetable broth or chicken broth
- 1 can (15 ounces) cannellini beans or kidney beans, drained and rinsed
- 1 cup chopped green beans (fresh or frozen)
- 1 cup small pasta (such as ditalini, elbow macaroni, or small shells), or rice
- 1 teaspoon dried thyme
- 1 teaspoon dried oregano
- 1 bay leaf
- Salt and pepper, to taste
- Grated Parmesan cheese, for serving
- Chopped fresh basil or parsley, for garnish (optional)

Instructions:

1. Sauté Aromatics: Heat olive oil in a large pot or Dutch oven over medium heat. Add diced onion and cook for 3-4 minutes until softened. Add minced garlic and cook for an additional minute until fragrant.
2. Add Vegetables: Add diced carrots, celery, zucchini, yellow squash, and potato to the pot. Sauté for 5-6 minutes, stirring occasionally, until vegetables begin to soften.
3. Add Tomatoes and Broth: Stir in diced tomatoes (with juices) and vegetable broth (or chicken broth). Bring to a simmer.
4. Simmer: Add cannellini beans (or kidney beans), chopped green beans, dried thyme, dried oregano, bay leaf, salt, and pepper. Stir well to combine. Reduce heat to low, cover, and simmer for 20-25 minutes, or until vegetables are tender and flavors have melded.
5. Add Pasta or Rice: If using pasta, add it to the pot and simmer for an additional 8-10 minutes, or until pasta is al dente. If using rice, add it earlier during the vegetable cooking stage and adjust cooking time according to package instructions.
6. Adjust Seasoning: Taste and adjust seasoning with more salt and pepper if needed. Remove bay leaf before serving.
7. Serve: Ladle minestrone soup into bowls. Sprinkle grated Parmesan cheese over each serving and garnish with chopped fresh basil or parsley if desired.

8. Enjoy: Serve minestrone soup hot, accompanied by crusty bread or a side salad for a complete meal.

Minestrone soup is versatile, so feel free to adjust the vegetables and herbs based on what you have on hand or personal preference. It's nutritious, filling, and perfect for warming up on cold days or anytime you crave a comforting bowl of soup.

BBQ pulled pork sandwiches

Ingredients:

For the Pulled Pork:

- 3-4 lbs pork shoulder (also known as pork butt), boneless
- 1 tablespoon olive oil
- Salt and pepper, to taste
- 1 cup BBQ sauce (store-bought or homemade)

For the Sandwiches:

- Hamburger buns or sandwich rolls
- Coleslaw (optional, for topping)
- Pickles (optional, for serving)

Instructions:

1. Prepare the Pork Shoulder:
    - Preheat oven to 300°F (150°C).
    - Pat dry the pork shoulder with paper towels. Season generously with salt and pepper.
    - In a large oven-safe pot or Dutch oven, heat olive oil over medium-high heat. Sear the pork shoulder on all sides until browned, about 3-4 minutes per side.
2. Slow Cook the Pork:
    - Remove the pork shoulder from the pot and set aside. Pour off any excess fat from the pot.
    - Return the pork shoulder to the pot. Pour BBQ sauce over the pork, turning to coat evenly.
    - Cover the pot with a lid or aluminum foil. Transfer to the preheated oven and bake for 3-4 hours, or until the pork is very tender and easily pulls apart with a fork.
3. Shred the Pork:
    - Remove the pot from the oven. Use two forks to shred the pork directly in the pot, mixing it with the BBQ sauce.
4. Assemble the Sandwiches:
    - Toast the hamburger buns or sandwich rolls if desired.
    - Spoon a generous amount of BBQ pulled pork onto the bottom half of each bun.
    - Top with coleslaw and pickles if using.
5. Serve:
    - Serve BBQ pulled pork sandwiches immediately while warm.
    - Enjoy with additional BBQ sauce on the side if desired.

BBQ pulled pork sandwiches are wonderfully flavorful and can be customized with your favorite toppings and sides. They are perfect for casual meals, parties, or any occasion where you want to enjoy delicious, tender pulled pork packed with smoky BBQ flavor.

Shrimp scampi with pasta

Ingredients:

- 12 ounces linguine or spaghetti
- 1 lb large shrimp, peeled and deveined
- 4 tablespoons unsalted butter
- 4 tablespoons olive oil
- 4 cloves garlic, minced
- 1/2 cup dry white wine (such as Sauvignon Blanc or Pinot Grigio)
- Juice of 1 lemon
- Zest of 1 lemon
- 1/4 teaspoon red pepper flakes (optional, for heat)
- Salt and pepper, to taste
- 1/4 cup chopped fresh parsley
- Grated Parmesan cheese, for serving
- Lemon wedges, for serving

Instructions:

1. Cook Pasta: Cook the linguine or spaghetti according to package instructions in a large pot of salted boiling water until al dente. Drain and set aside, reserving about 1/2 cup of pasta water.
2. Prepare Shrimp: While the pasta is cooking, pat the shrimp dry with paper towels. Season lightly with salt and pepper.
3. Sauté Shrimp: In a large skillet or frying pan, heat 2 tablespoons of butter and 2 tablespoons of olive oil over medium-high heat. Add the shrimp in a single layer and cook for 2-3 minutes per side, or until shrimp are pink and opaque. Remove shrimp from the skillet and set aside.
4. Make Garlic Butter Sauce: In the same skillet, add remaining butter and olive oil. Add minced garlic and red pepper flakes (if using). Sauté for 1-2 minutes until garlic is fragrant and lightly golden.
5. Deglaze with Wine: Pour in white wine, lemon juice, and lemon zest. Bring to a simmer and cook for 2-3 minutes, stirring occasionally, until slightly reduced.
6. Combine Pasta and Sauce: Add the cooked pasta to the skillet with the garlic butter sauce. Toss well to coat the pasta evenly with the sauce. If the sauce seems too dry, add a splash of reserved pasta water to loosen it.
7. Add Shrimp and Parsley: Add the cooked shrimp back to the skillet. Toss gently to combine with the pasta and sauce. Stir in chopped parsley.
8. Season and Serve: Taste and adjust seasoning with salt and pepper if needed. Serve shrimp scampi over pasta immediately, garnished with grated Parmesan cheese and lemon wedges.
9. Enjoy: Serve shrimp scampi with pasta hot, accompanied by a side salad and crusty bread if desired.

Shrimp scampi with pasta is a delicious and elegant dish that is perfect for a special dinner or entertaining guests. The combination of tender shrimp, garlic butter sauce, and pasta creates a flavorful and satisfying meal that is sure to impress!

Chicken quesadillas

Ingredients:

- 2 cups cooked chicken breast, shredded or diced
- 1 cup shredded Monterey Jack cheese or Mexican blend cheese
- 1/2 cup diced bell peppers (any color)
- 1/4 cup diced onion
- 1 teaspoon chili powder
- 1/2 teaspoon ground cumin
- 1/2 teaspoon garlic powder
- Salt and pepper, to taste
- 4 large flour tortillas (burrito size)
- 2 tablespoons vegetable oil or olive oil
- Optional toppings: Salsa, sour cream, guacamole, chopped cilantro

Instructions:

1. Prepare Chicken: If chicken breast is not cooked, boil, bake, or grill it until fully cooked, then shred or dice into small pieces.
2. Season Chicken: In a bowl, combine shredded chicken with chili powder, ground cumin, garlic powder, salt, and pepper. Mix well to coat the chicken evenly with the spices.
3. Assemble Quesadillas: Lay out the flour tortillas on a clean surface. Divide the shredded cheese evenly among the tortillas, spreading it over one half of each tortilla.
4. Add Chicken and Veggies: Distribute the seasoned chicken evenly over the cheese on each tortilla. Sprinkle diced bell peppers and onions over the chicken.
5. Fold Tortillas: Fold the tortillas in half over the filling to create half-moon shapes.
6. Cook Quesadillas: Heat 1 tablespoon of oil in a large skillet over medium heat. Place 1 or 2 quesadillas (depending on the size of your skillet) in the skillet and cook for 2-3 minutes on each side, or until golden brown and crispy, and the cheese is melted. Repeat with remaining quesadillas, adding more oil if needed.
7. Serve: Remove quesadillas from the skillet and cut each into wedges using a pizza cutter or a sharp knife. Serve hot with optional toppings such as salsa, sour cream, guacamole, or chopped cilantro.
8. Enjoy: Enjoy your homemade chicken quesadillas as a delicious snack, lunch, or dinner!

These chicken quesadillas are versatile, and you can customize them by adding additional ingredients like black beans, corn, or jalapeños. They are quick to make and perfect for feeding a crowd or enjoying a cozy meal at home.

Ratatouille

Ingredients:

- 1 eggplant, diced into 1-inch cubes
- 2 zucchini, diced into 1-inch cubes
- 1 yellow bell pepper, diced
- 1 red bell pepper, diced
- 1 onion, diced
- 3 cloves garlic, minced
- 4 tomatoes, diced
- 2 tablespoons tomato paste
- 1/4 cup olive oil
- 1 teaspoon dried thyme
- 1 teaspoon dried oregano
- Salt and pepper, to taste
- Fresh basil leaves, chopped, for garnish

Instructions:

1. Prepare Vegetables: Start by preparing all the vegetables. Dice the eggplant, zucchini, bell peppers, onion, and tomatoes into similar-sized cubes.
2. Sauté Onion and Garlic: In a large pot or Dutch oven, heat olive oil over medium heat. Add diced onion and sauté for 3-4 minutes until softened. Add minced garlic and cook for an additional minute until fragrant.
3. Cook Vegetables: Add diced eggplant, zucchini, and bell peppers to the pot. Cook for 8-10 minutes, stirring occasionally, until vegetables start to soften.
4. Add Tomatoes and Tomato Paste: Stir in diced tomatoes and tomato paste. Mix well to combine with the vegetables.
5. Season: Add dried thyme, dried oregano, salt, and pepper to taste. Stir to incorporate the seasonings.
6. Simmer: Reduce heat to low, cover the pot, and let the ratatouille simmer gently for 20-25 minutes, stirring occasionally, until all vegetables are tender and flavors have melded together.
7. Adjust Seasoning: Taste and adjust seasoning with more salt and pepper if needed.
8. Serve: Remove ratatouille from heat. Garnish with chopped fresh basil leaves before serving.
9. Enjoy: Serve ratatouille warm as a side dish, over rice or pasta, or even on its own with crusty bread.

Ratatouille is a versatile dish that can be enjoyed hot, cold, or at room temperature. It's perfect for using up seasonal vegetables and can be made in advance, as its flavors tend to develop even more over time. This dish captures the essence of Mediterranean cuisine and is both healthy and delicious!

Eggplant Parmesan

Ingredients:

- 2 medium-sized eggplants, sliced into 1/2-inch rounds
- Salt, for sprinkling
- 1 cup all-purpose flour
- 3 large eggs, beaten
- 2 cups breadcrumbs (preferably Italian seasoned breadcrumbs)
- 1 cup grated Parmesan cheese, divided
- 2 cups marinara sauce (store-bought or homemade)
- 2 cups shredded mozzarella cheese
- 1/4 cup chopped fresh basil or parsley, for garnish
- Olive oil, for frying

Instructions:

1. Prep the Eggplant: Place the eggplant slices on a paper towel-lined baking sheet. Sprinkle both sides generously with salt. Let them sit for 20-30 minutes to release excess moisture. Pat dry with paper towels.
2. Set Up Breading Station: Prepare three shallow bowls. Place flour in the first bowl, beaten eggs in the second bowl, and breadcrumbs mixed with 1/2 cup grated Parmesan cheese in the third bowl.
3. Bread the Eggplant: Dredge each eggplant slice in the flour, shaking off excess. Dip into the beaten eggs, allowing excess to drip off. Coat evenly with the breadcrumb mixture, pressing gently to adhere. Place breaded eggplant slices on a baking sheet.
4. Fry the Eggplant: In a large skillet, heat enough olive oil over medium-high heat to generously coat the bottom of the pan. Fry the eggplant slices in batches until golden brown and crispy, about 2-3 minutes per side. Transfer to a paper towel-lined plate to drain excess oil.
5. Assemble the Eggplant Parmesan: Preheat the oven to 375°F (190°C). Spread 1 cup of marinara sauce evenly on the bottom of a 9x13-inch baking dish. Arrange a single layer of fried eggplant slices over the sauce. Spoon more marinara sauce over the eggplant, then sprinkle with shredded mozzarella cheese and grated Parmesan cheese. Repeat layers, finishing with a layer of marinara sauce and cheese on top.
6. Bake: Cover the baking dish loosely with aluminum foil. Bake in the preheated oven for 30 minutes. Remove the foil and bake for an additional 10-15 minutes, or until the cheese is melted and bubbly.
7. Rest and Garnish: Remove from the oven and let the Eggplant Parmesan rest for 5-10 minutes before serving. Garnish with chopped fresh basil or parsley.
8. Serve: Serve warm, either as a main dish with a side of pasta or a salad, or as a delicious appetizer.

Eggplant Parmesan is a comforting and satisfying dish that's perfect for a family dinner or entertaining guests. It's rich in flavor and texture, with the crispy eggplant complemented by the gooey cheese and tangy marinara sauce. Enjoy this classic Italian favorite!

Sushi rolls (vegetarian or with fish)

Ingredients:

- Sushi rice (2 cups uncooked rice, sushi rice vinegar, sugar, and salt for seasoning)
- Nori (seaweed sheets)
- Fillings (choose from vegetables like cucumber, avocado, carrot, bell pepper, or fish like salmon, tuna, or cooked shrimp)
- Soy sauce, pickled ginger, and wasabi (for serving)

Equipment:

- Bamboo sushi rolling mat (makisu)
- Plastic wrap (for covering the bamboo mat)
- Sharp knife (preferably a sushi knife or a very sharp chef's knife)

Instructions:

1. Prepare Sushi Rice:
    - Rinse sushi rice under cold water until the water runs clear.
    - Cook rice according to package instructions or in a rice cooker. Once cooked, let it cool slightly.
    - In a small bowl, mix sushi rice vinegar (seasoned with sugar and salt) into the rice. Allow it to cool to room temperature.
2. Prepare Fillings:
    - Slice vegetables into thin strips (julienne) or into thin slices.
    - If using fish, ensure it's sushi-grade and sliced thinly.
3. Prepare Bamboo Mat:
    - Place a bamboo sushi rolling mat on a clean surface.
    - Cover the mat with plastic wrap to prevent rice from sticking.
4. Assemble Sushi Rolls:
    - Lay a sheet of nori, shiny side down, on the plastic-covered bamboo mat.
    - Wet your hands with water to prevent rice from sticking. Spread a thin layer of sushi rice evenly over the nori, leaving about 1-inch of nori uncovered at the top.
5. Add Fillings:
    - Arrange your choice of fillings in a line across the center of the rice-covered nori sheet.
6. Roll Sushi:
    - Using the bamboo mat, start rolling the sushi away from you, using gentle pressure to shape it into a cylinder.
    - Continue rolling until you reach the uncovered edge of the nori.
    - Moisten the edge of the nori with water to seal the roll.
7. Slice and Serve:

- Use a sharp knife to slice the sushi roll into bite-sized pieces, wiping the knife clean with a damp cloth between cuts.
- Arrange sushi pieces on a plate and serve with soy sauce, pickled ginger, and wasabi.

Vegetarian Sushi Roll Ideas:

- Avocado Cucumber Roll: Sliced avocado and cucumber.
- Vegetable Roll: Carrot, cucumber, bell pepper, and avocado.
- Tempura Vegetable Roll: Tempura-fried sweet potato, avocado, and cucumber.

Fish Sushi Roll Ideas:

- California Roll: Crab (or imitation crab), avocado, and cucumber.
- Salmon Avocado Roll: Fresh salmon and avocado.
- Spicy Tuna Roll: Spicy tuna filling (tuna mixed with spicy mayo) and cucumber.

Tips:

- Keep Hands Moist: Keep a bowl of water nearby to keep hands moist when handling sushi rice.
- Use Fresh Ingredients: Ensure fillings are fresh and sliced thinly for easy rolling.
- Experiment: Don't be afraid to experiment with different fillings and combinations to suit your taste.

Making sushi rolls at home allows for creativity and customization, whether you prefer vegetarian options or enjoy seafood. With practice, you'll master the art of rolling sushi and enjoy delicious homemade sushi whenever you crave it!

Lentil soup

Ingredients:

- 1 cup dried lentils (brown or green), rinsed and picked over
- 1 tablespoon olive oil
- 1 onion, chopped
- 2 carrots, diced
- 2 celery stalks, diced
- 3 cloves garlic, minced
- 1 teaspoon ground cumin
- 1 teaspoon ground coriander
- 1/2 teaspoon smoked paprika (optional)
- 6 cups vegetable broth or chicken broth
- 1 bay leaf
- Salt and pepper, to taste
- Juice of 1 lemon (optional, for added brightness)
- Fresh parsley or cilantro, chopped, for garnish (optional)

Instructions:

1. Prepare Lentils: Rinse the lentils under cold water and pick out any debris or stones. Set aside.
2. Sauté Aromatics: Heat olive oil in a large pot or Dutch oven over medium heat. Add chopped onion, diced carrots, and diced celery. Sauté for 5-6 minutes, or until vegetables start to soften.
3. Add Garlic and Spices: Add minced garlic, ground cumin, ground coriander, and smoked paprika (if using). Cook for 1 minute, stirring constantly, until fragrant.
4. Cook Lentils: Add the rinsed lentils to the pot. Stir to combine with the vegetables and spices.
5. Add Broth and Bay Leaf: Pour in the vegetable broth or chicken broth. Add the bay leaf. Bring to a boil.
6. Simmer: Reduce heat to low, cover, and simmer for 30-35 minutes, or until lentils are tender. Stir occasionally.
7. Season: Taste and season with salt and pepper to taste. Add more broth or water if you prefer a thinner soup consistency.
8. Finish: If using, squeeze in the juice of 1 lemon for added brightness. Stir to combine.
9. Serve: Ladle lentil soup into bowls. Garnish with chopped fresh parsley or cilantro, if desired.
10. Enjoy: Serve lentil soup hot, accompanied by crusty bread or a side salad for a complete meal.

Tips:

- Variations: You can add diced potatoes, chopped spinach or kale, or even diced tomatoes for additional flavor and texture.
- Storage: Lentil soup keeps well in the refrigerator for up to 4-5 days and can also be frozen for longer storage. Reheat gently on the stove or in the microwave.
- Customization: Adjust the seasoning and spices to your preference. You can also blend a portion of the soup with an immersion blender for a creamier texture.

Lentil soup is nutritious, filling, and budget-friendly, making it a perfect option for lunch or dinner. It's also versatile, allowing you to customize it with your favorite vegetables and spices. Enjoy this comforting lentil soup any time of the year!

Stuffed baked apples

Ingredients:

- 4 large apples (such as Honeycrisp, Gala, or Fuji)
- 1/2 cup old-fashioned oats
- 1/4 cup brown sugar
- 1 teaspoon cinnamon
- 1/4 teaspoon nutmeg
- 1/4 cup chopped nuts (such as walnuts, pecans, or almonds)
- 1/4 cup raisins or dried cranberries
- 2 tablespoons unsalted butter, cut into small pieces
- 1/4 cup apple juice or water
- Optional: vanilla ice cream or whipped cream, for serving

Instructions:

1. Preheat Oven: Preheat your oven to 375°F (190°C).
2. Prepare Apples:
    - Wash and core the apples, leaving the bottom intact so the filling doesn't spill out. You can use an apple corer or a paring knife to remove the cores. Be careful not to cut all the way through the bottom.
    - If desired, you can cut a small slice off the bottom of each apple to help them sit upright.
3. Mix Filling:
    - In a bowl, combine old-fashioned oats, brown sugar, cinnamon, nutmeg, chopped nuts, and raisins or dried cranberries. Mix well.
    - Stuff the apple cores with the oat mixture, pressing it in gently.
4. Arrange Apples:
    - Place the stuffed apples in a baking dish. Dot each apple with small pieces of butter and pour the apple juice or water into the bottom of the dish.
5. Bake:
    - Cover the baking dish with aluminum foil and bake in the preheated oven for about 30 minutes. Then, remove the foil and continue baking for an additional 15-20 minutes, or until the apples are tender and the filling is golden brown.
6. Serve:
    - Allow the apples to cool slightly before serving. Top with a scoop of vanilla ice cream or a dollop of whipped cream, if desired.
7. Enjoy: Serve warm and enjoy the delightful combination of soft apples, sweet filling, and a touch of spice.

Tips:

- Choosing Apples: Firm, crisp apples work best for baking. Avoid varieties that are too soft.
- Variations: You can add a drizzle of maple syrup, a sprinkle of granola, or a handful of fresh berries to the filling for extra flavor and texture.
- Storage: Leftover baked apples can be stored in the refrigerator for up to 3 days. Reheat them in the microwave or oven before serving.

Stuffed baked apples are a cozy, satisfying dessert that's easy to prepare and sure to impress. Enjoy the warm, spiced flavors with a scoop of ice cream or a drizzle of caramel sauce for an extra touch of sweetness!

Falafel wraps

Ingredients:

For the Falafel:

- 1 cup dried chickpeas, soaked overnight (or canned chickpeas, drained and rinsed)
- 1/2 onion, roughly chopped
- 3 cloves garlic
- 1/4 cup fresh parsley, chopped
- 1/4 cup fresh cilantro, chopped
- 1 teaspoon ground cumin
- 1 teaspoon ground coriander
- 1/4 teaspoon cayenne pepper (optional)
- 1 teaspoon salt
- 1/2 teaspoon black pepper
- 1 tablespoon all-purpose flour (optional, for binding)
- 1 teaspoon baking powder
- Vegetable oil, for frying

For Assembling Wraps:

- Whole wheat or regular flour tortillas
- Hummus
- Tzatziki sauce or yogurt sauce (see recipe below)
- Sliced tomatoes
- Sliced cucumbers
- Shredded lettuce or mixed greens
- Sliced red onion
- Sliced pickles or pickled turnips (optional)
- Lemon wedges, for serving

For Tzatziki Sauce:

- 1 cup Greek yogurt
- 1/2 cucumber, peeled, seeded, and grated
- 2 cloves garlic, minced
- 1 tablespoon lemon juice
- 1 tablespoon chopped fresh dill (or 1 teaspoon dried dill)
- Salt and pepper, to taste

Instructions:

1. Make the Falafel:

1. Prepare Chickpeas: If using dried chickpeas, drain and rinse them after soaking overnight. Pat them dry with paper towels.
2. Blend Ingredients: In a food processor, combine chickpeas, onion, garlic, parsley, cilantro, cumin, coriander, cayenne pepper (if using), salt, and black pepper. Pulse until mixture is finely ground but not pureed.
3. Add Binding Ingredients: Sprinkle baking powder and flour (if using) over the mixture. Pulse a few more times until combined. The mixture should hold together when squeezed.
4. Form Falafel: Scoop out tablespoon-sized portions of the mixture and form into small patties or balls. Place them on a baking sheet lined with parchment paper.
5. Fry Falafel: In a large skillet, heat vegetable oil over medium-high heat. Fry falafel in batches for 2-3 minutes per side, or until golden brown and crispy. Transfer to a plate lined with paper towels to drain excess oil.

2. Make Tzatziki Sauce:

1. Prepare Cucumber: Grate cucumber using a box grater. Squeeze grated cucumber with your hands to remove excess moisture.
2. Mix Ingredients: In a bowl, combine Greek yogurt, grated cucumber, minced garlic, lemon juice, chopped dill, salt, and pepper. Stir well to combine. Adjust seasoning to taste.

3. Assemble Falafel Wraps:

1. Warm Tortillas: Heat tortillas in a dry skillet or microwave until warm and pliable.
2. Spread Hummus: Spread a generous layer of hummus onto each tortilla.
3. Add Toppings: Place 2-3 falafel patties on top of the hummus. Add sliced tomatoes, cucumbers, shredded lettuce, red onion, and pickles or pickled turnips (if using).
4. Drizzle with Tzatziki: Spoon tzatziki sauce or yogurt sauce over the toppings.
5. Wrap and Serve: Fold the sides of the tortilla over the fillings, then roll tightly to form a wrap. Cut in half diagonally if desired. Serve falafel wraps immediately with lemon wedges on the side.

Tips:

- Make Ahead: Falafel mixture can be prepared ahead and refrigerated until ready to fry. Leftover falafel can also be stored in the refrigerator and reheated in a toaster oven or skillet.
- Variations: Customize your wraps with your favorite toppings such as olives, feta cheese, or hot sauce.
- Gluten-Free Option: Use gluten-free flour and serve falafel in lettuce wraps or gluten-free tortillas.

Falafel wraps are a delicious way to enjoy the flavors of the Middle East in a convenient handheld meal. They are packed with protein, vegetables, and flavorful sauces, making them a healthy and satisfying choice for any occasion!

Baked tilapia with vegetables

Ingredients:

- 4 tilapia fillets (about 6 ounces each)
- 2 tablespoons olive oil
- 2 cloves garlic, minced
- 1 teaspoon dried thyme (or use other herbs like rosemary or basil)
- Salt and pepper, to taste
- Juice of 1 lemon
- 1 zucchini, sliced
- 1 yellow squash, sliced
- 1 bell pepper (any color), sliced
- 1 cup cherry tomatoes, halved
- Fresh parsley or basil, chopped, for garnish
- Lemon wedges, for serving

Instructions:

1. Preheat Oven: Preheat your oven to 400°F (200°C).
2. Prepare Tilapia and Vegetables:
   - Pat dry the tilapia fillets with paper towels and place them on a large baking sheet lined with parchment paper or foil.
   - In a bowl, toss the sliced zucchini, yellow squash, bell pepper, and cherry tomatoes with olive oil, minced garlic, dried thyme, salt, and pepper.
3. Season and Arrange: Drizzle the tilapia fillets with a little olive oil and lemon juice. Season with salt and pepper.
4. Bake: Arrange the seasoned vegetables around the tilapia fillets on the baking sheet. Bake in the preheated oven for 12-15 minutes, or until the fish is cooked through and flakes easily with a fork.
5. Garnish and Serve: Remove from the oven and garnish with chopped fresh parsley or basil. Serve baked tilapia and vegetables hot, with lemon wedges on the side.

Tips:

- Variations: Feel free to use other vegetables such as broccoli, asparagus, or green beans. Adjust baking time accordingly depending on the vegetables used.
- Seasoning: You can customize the seasoning for the tilapia with your favorite herbs and spices. Lemon pepper seasoning or paprika also work well.
- Serve: Baked tilapia with vegetables pairs well with rice, quinoa, or crusty bread. It's a complete meal in itself!

Baked tilapia with vegetables is a nutritious and delicious dish that's quick to prepare, making it perfect for busy weeknights or a healthy family dinner. Enjoy the tender fish and vibrant vegetables with minimal effort and maximum flavor!

Chicken and vegetable kebabs

Ingredients:

- 1 lb (450g) boneless, skinless chicken breasts or thighs, cut into 1-inch cubes
- 1 red bell pepper, cut into 1-inch pieces
- 1 yellow bell pepper, cut into 1-inch pieces
- 1 red onion, cut into 1-inch pieces
- 1 zucchini, sliced into rounds
- Cherry tomatoes
- 8-10 wooden or metal skewers

For the Marinade:

- 1/4 cup olive oil
- 2 tablespoons soy sauce
- 2 tablespoons lemon juice (about 1 lemon)
- 2 cloves garlic, minced
- 1 teaspoon dried oregano
- 1 teaspoon paprika
- 1/2 teaspoon ground cumin
- Salt and pepper, to taste

Instructions:

1. Prepare Skewers:
    - If using wooden skewers, soak them in water for at least 30 minutes to prevent them from burning during cooking.
    - Preheat your grill to medium-high heat or preheat your oven to 400°F (200°C).
2. Make Marinade:
    - In a small bowl, whisk together olive oil, soy sauce, lemon juice, minced garlic, dried oregano, paprika, ground cumin, salt, and pepper.
3. Marinate Chicken:
    - Place the chicken cubes in a bowl or shallow dish. Pour half of the marinade over the chicken, reserving the other half for the vegetables. Toss the chicken to coat evenly. Let it marinate for at least 15-30 minutes in the refrigerator.
4. Prepare Vegetables:
    - In another bowl, toss the bell peppers, red onion, zucchini, and cherry tomatoes with the remaining marinade.
5. Assemble Kebabs:
    - Thread the marinated chicken, bell peppers, red onion, zucchini slices, and cherry tomatoes onto the skewers, alternating between ingredients.
6. Grill or Bake:
    - Grill the kebabs over medium-high heat for 10-12 minutes, turning occasionally, until the chicken is fully cooked and the vegetables are tender and lightly charred.

- Alternatively, arrange the assembled kebabs on a baking sheet lined with foil and bake in the preheated oven for 15-20 minutes, or until chicken is cooked through and vegetables are tender.
7. Serve:
    - Remove kebabs from the grill or oven and let them rest for a few minutes. Serve hot, garnished with chopped parsley or cilantro if desired.

Tips:

- Additional Ingredients: Feel free to add other vegetables such as mushrooms, eggplant, or chunks of pineapple for extra flavor and variety.
- Serve with: Serve chicken and vegetable kebabs with rice, quinoa, or a fresh salad. They also pair well with tzatziki sauce or a yogurt-based dressing.
- Variations: You can also use shrimp or beef cubes instead of chicken for different variations of kebabs.

Chicken and vegetable kebabs are a versatile dish that's perfect for outdoor grilling or indoor baking. They are colorful, flavorful, and make a healthy and satisfying meal for any occasion!

Tortellini with pesto sauce

Ingredients:

- 1 lb (450g) cheese or spinach tortellini (fresh or frozen)
- 1/2 cup basil pesto (store-bought or homemade)
- 1/4 cup grated Parmesan cheese
- Salt and pepper, to taste
- Fresh basil leaves, chopped, for garnish (optional)

Instructions:

1. Cook Tortellini:
    - Bring a large pot of salted water to a boil. Cook the tortellini according to the package instructions until they are al dente (usually about 2-3 minutes for fresh tortellini or 7-10 minutes for frozen).
2. Prepare Pesto Sauce:
    - While the tortellini is cooking, warm the pesto sauce in a large skillet over low heat. If the pesto is too thick, you can thin it out with a little pasta cooking water.
3. Combine Tortellini and Pesto:
    - Drain the cooked tortellini, reserving a cup of pasta cooking water. Add the drained tortellini directly to the skillet with the warmed pesto sauce. Toss gently to coat the tortellini evenly with the pesto. If needed, add a splash of pasta cooking water to loosen the sauce.
4. Season and Serve:
    - Stir in grated Parmesan cheese and season with salt and pepper to taste. Garnish with chopped fresh basil leaves if desired.
5. Serve Warm:
    - Serve tortellini with pesto sauce immediately, garnished with extra Parmesan cheese and basil if desired.

Tips:

- Homemade Pesto: If making homemade pesto, blend together fresh basil leaves, garlic, pine nuts (or walnuts), Parmesan cheese, and olive oil in a food processor until smooth. Adjust seasoning to taste.
- Variations: You can add cooked chicken, shrimp, or vegetables like cherry tomatoes or spinach to make it a heartier meal.
- Storage: Leftover tortellini with pesto sauce can be stored in an airtight container in the refrigerator for up to 3 days. Reheat gently on the stove or in the microwave, adding a splash of water to refresh the sauce.

Tortellini with pesto sauce is a simple yet flavorful dish that's perfect for a quick weeknight dinner or a special occasion. Enjoy the rich, herbaceous flavors of basil pesto paired with tender tortellini for a satisfying meal!

Veggie stir-fry noodles

Ingredients:

- 8 oz (225g) noodles (such as spaghetti, udon, rice noodles, or soba noodles)
- 2 tablespoons sesame oil (or vegetable oil)

- 2 cloves garlic, minced
- 1-inch piece of ginger, minced or grated
- 1 bell pepper, thinly sliced
- 1 carrot, julienned or thinly sliced
- 1 small zucchini, thinly sliced
- 1 cup broccoli florets
- 1 cup snap peas or snow peas, trimmed
- 1/2 cup sliced mushrooms (optional)
- 1/4 cup soy sauce (use tamari for gluten-free)
- 2 tablespoons oyster sauce (optional, omit for vegetarian/vegan)
- 1 tablespoon rice vinegar or white vinegar
- 1 tablespoon brown sugar or honey
- Salt and pepper, to taste
- Crushed red pepper flakes (optional, for heat)
- Fresh cilantro or green onions, chopped, for garnish (optional)
- Sesame seeds, for garnish (optional)

Instructions:

1. **Cook Noodles:**
   - Cook the noodles according to the package instructions until al dente. Drain and rinse under cold water to stop cooking. Set aside.
2. **Prepare Stir-Fry Sauce:**
   - In a small bowl, whisk together soy sauce, oyster sauce (if using), rice vinegar, brown sugar or honey, and a pinch of salt and pepper. Set aside.
3. **Stir-Fry Vegetables:**
   - Heat sesame oil in a large skillet or wok over medium-high heat. Add minced garlic and ginger, and sauté for about 30 seconds until fragrant.
   - Add bell pepper, carrot, zucchini, broccoli florets, snap peas, and mushrooms (if using). Stir-fry for 4-5 minutes, or until vegetables are tender-crisp.
4. **Combine Noodles and Sauce:**
   - Add the cooked noodles to the skillet with the stir-fried vegetables. Pour the prepared stir-fry sauce over the noodles and vegetables. Toss everything together gently to coat evenly with the sauce.
5. **Finish and Serve:**
   - Cook for another 1-2 minutes until heated through. Taste and adjust seasoning if needed. If you like it spicy, sprinkle with crushed red pepper flakes.
   - Garnish with chopped cilantro or green onions, and sesame seeds if desired.
6. **Serve Warm:**
   - Serve veggie stir-fry noodles immediately, while hot. Enjoy as a complete meal or as a side dish.

Tips:

- Vegetable Variations: Feel free to customize with your favorite vegetables such as cabbage, baby corn, bean sprouts, or spinach.
- Protein Addition: Add cooked tofu, shrimp, chicken, or beef strips for added protein.
- Make It Gluten-Free: Use gluten-free noodles and tamari instead of soy sauce.

Veggie stir-fry noodles are a versatile and satisfying dish that's perfect for a quick weeknight dinner. With colorful vegetables and a flavorful sauce, this dish is sure to become a favorite in your home!

Tofu tacos

Ingredients:

For the Tofu:

- 1 block (14-16 oz) extra-firm tofu

- 2 tablespoons soy sauce or tamari
- 1 tablespoon lime juice
- 1 tablespoon olive oil or vegetable oil
- 1 teaspoon chili powder
- 1/2 teaspoon ground cumin
- 1/2 teaspoon paprika
- 1/4 teaspoon garlic powder
- Salt and pepper, to taste

For the Tacos:

- 8 small corn or flour tortillas
- 1 cup shredded lettuce or cabbage
- 1 avocado, sliced or mashed
- 1/2 cup salsa or pico de gallo
- Fresh cilantro, chopped, for garnish
- Lime wedges, for serving

Instructions:

1. Prepare the Tofu:
    - Press the tofu: Wrap the block of tofu in paper towels and place it between two plates. Place a heavy object (like a can or book) on top of the plate to press out excess moisture from the tofu for about 15-20 minutes.
    - Cut the pressed tofu into small cubes or strips.
    - In a bowl, whisk together soy sauce (or tamari), lime juice, olive oil, chili powder, cumin, paprika, garlic powder, salt, and pepper.
    - Add the tofu cubes to the marinade and gently toss to coat. Let it marinate for at least 15-20 minutes, or longer if time allows.
2. Cook the Tofu:
    - Heat a large skillet or non-stick pan over medium-high heat. Add the marinated tofu cubes (reserve any leftover marinade) and cook for 5-7 minutes, stirring occasionally, until tofu is browned and crispy on all sides. If the tofu starts to stick, you can add a little more oil or a splash of water.
    - Pour the reserved marinade over the tofu and cook for another 1-2 minutes, stirring constantly, until the sauce thickens and coats the tofu. Remove from heat.
3. Assemble the Tacos:
    - Warm the tortillas: Heat the tortillas in a dry skillet or microwave until warm and pliable.
    - Assemble each taco with a layer of shredded lettuce or cabbage, followed by a portion of the cooked tofu.
    - Top with avocado slices or mashed avocado, salsa or pico de gallo, and chopped cilantro.
    - Serve tofu tacos with lime wedges on the side for squeezing over the tacos.

Tips:

- Variations: Customize your tofu tacos with additional toppings such as shredded cheese, sour cream or Greek yogurt, diced tomatoes, black beans, or corn.
- Spice Level: Adjust the amount of chili powder or add hot sauce to suit your taste preference.
- Make It Vegan: Ensure the tortillas and toppings are vegan-friendly. Skip dairy-based toppings and use vegan salsa or pico de gallo.

Tofu tacos are a flavorful and satisfying vegetarian option that's perfect for Taco Tuesdays or any day of the week. Enjoy the crunchy texture of the tofu combined with fresh toppings for a delicious meal!

Lemon garlic shrimp with couscous

Ingredients:

For the Lemon Garlic Shrimp:

- 1 lb (450g) large shrimp, peeled and deveined
- 3 cloves garlic, minced

- Zest and juice of 1 lemon
- 2 tablespoons olive oil
- Salt and pepper, to taste
- Crushed red pepper flakes (optional)
- Fresh parsley, chopped, for garnish

For the Couscous:

- 1 cup couscous
- 1 1/4 cups chicken or vegetable broth (or water)
- 1 tablespoon butter or olive oil
- Salt, to taste

Instructions:

For the Lemon Garlic Shrimp:

1. Marinate Shrimp:
    - In a bowl, combine shrimp with minced garlic, lemon zest, lemon juice, olive oil, salt, pepper, and crushed red pepper flakes (if using). Toss well to coat the shrimp evenly. Let marinate for about 10-15 minutes.
2. Cook Shrimp:
    - Heat a large skillet over medium-high heat. Add the marinated shrimp in a single layer (work in batches if needed). Cook for 2-3 minutes per side, or until shrimp are pink and cooked through. Be careful not to overcook, as shrimp can become tough.
3. Garnish:
    - Sprinkle chopped fresh parsley over the cooked shrimp for garnish. Remove from heat and set aside.

For the Couscous:

1. Prepare Couscous:
    - In a saucepan, bring the chicken or vegetable broth (or water) and butter or olive oil to a boil.
2. Cook Couscous:
    - Stir in the couscous and a pinch of salt. Remove from heat, cover, and let it sit for 5 minutes. Fluff with a fork to separate the grains.

To Serve:

- Divide the couscous among serving plates or bowls.
- Top with the lemon garlic shrimp.
- Drizzle any remaining pan juices from the shrimp over the couscous.
- Garnish with additional chopped parsley and lemon wedges if desired.

Tips:

- Vegetable Addition: You can add sautéed vegetables such as bell peppers, zucchini, or spinach to the couscous for added flavor and nutrients.
- Storage: Store any leftover lemon garlic shrimp and couscous separately in airtight containers in the refrigerator. Reheat gently in the microwave or skillet before serving.

This lemon garlic shrimp with couscous is a light yet satisfying dish that's perfect for a quick weeknight dinner or a special occasion. Enjoy the bright flavors of lemon and garlic combined with tender shrimp and fluffy couscous!

Black bean burgers

Ingredients:

- 2 cans (15 oz each) black beans, drained and rinsed (or 3 cups cooked black beans)
- 1/2 cup finely chopped onion
- 1/2 cup rolled oats or breadcrumbs
- 1/4 cup chopped fresh cilantro or parsley
- 2 cloves garlic, minced
- 1 teaspoon ground cumin

- 1 teaspoon chili powder
- 1/2 teaspoon smoked paprika (optional)
- Salt and pepper, to taste
- 1 tablespoon soy sauce or tamari
- 1 tablespoon olive oil (plus more for cooking)
- 1 tablespoon lime juice
- 1 egg (or flax egg for vegan option)
- Burger buns
- Toppings: lettuce, tomato slices, avocado, cheese slices, etc.

Instructions:

1. Mash the Black Beans:
   - In a large bowl, mash half of the black beans with a fork or potato masher until mostly smooth. Leave the other half of the beans whole or lightly mashed for texture.
2. Mix Ingredients:
   - Add finely chopped onion, rolled oats or breadcrumbs, chopped cilantro or parsley, minced garlic, ground cumin, chili powder, smoked paprika (if using), salt, pepper, soy sauce or tamari, olive oil, lime juice, and egg (or flax egg) to the mashed black beans. Mix until well combined.
3. Form Patties:
   - Divide the mixture into 4-6 equal portions, depending on how large you want your burgers. Shape each portion into a patty about 1/2 to 3/4 inch thick. If the mixture is too wet to handle, you can add a bit more oats or breadcrumbs to help bind it.
4. Cook the Burgers:
   - Heat a tablespoon of olive oil in a skillet over medium-high heat. Once hot, add the patties (in batches if necessary) and cook for 4-5 minutes on each side, or until golden brown and heated through. Alternatively, you can bake the patties in a preheated oven at 375°F (190°C) for 20-25 minutes, flipping halfway through.
5. Serve:
   - Toast the burger buns lightly if desired. Place a black bean patty on each bun and add your favorite toppings such as lettuce, tomato slices, avocado, cheese, or condiments.
6. Enjoy:
   - Serve black bean burgers immediately while warm. Enjoy the homemade goodness!

Tips:

- Make Ahead: You can prepare the black bean burger patties in advance and refrigerate them for up to 24 hours before cooking.

- Freezing: You can also freeze uncooked patties between layers of parchment paper in an airtight container for up to 3 months. Thaw in the refrigerator overnight before cooking.
- Customize: Feel free to adjust the seasonings and add-ins according to your preference. Some people like to add diced bell peppers, corn kernels, or jalapeños for extra flavor and texture.

These homemade black bean burgers are nutritious, packed with protein and fiber, and incredibly flavorful. They make a great alternative to meat-based burgers and are sure to be a hit at your next meal!

Mushroom risotto

Ingredients:

- 1 cup Arborio rice
- 4 cups vegetable or chicken broth (preferably warm)
- 1/2 cup dry white wine (optional)
- 2 tablespoons olive oil or unsalted butter

- 1 small onion, finely chopped
- 2 cloves garlic, minced
- 8 oz (225g) mushrooms (such as cremini, shiitake, or button), sliced
- 1/2 cup grated Parmesan cheese
- Salt and freshly ground black pepper, to taste
- Fresh parsley, chopped, for garnish (optional)

Instructions:

1. **Prepare the Broth:**
   - Heat the vegetable or chicken broth in a saucepan over medium heat. Keep it warm throughout the cooking process.
2. **Sauté Mushrooms:**
   - In a large skillet or wide saucepan, heat 1 tablespoon of olive oil or butter over medium heat. Add the sliced mushrooms and cook until they are golden brown and any liquid released has evaporated, about 5-7 minutes. Season with salt and pepper. Remove the mushrooms from the skillet and set aside.
3. **Cook Onion and Garlic:**
   - In the same skillet, heat the remaining tablespoon of olive oil or butter over medium heat. Add the finely chopped onion and cook until it becomes translucent, about 3-4 minutes. Add the minced garlic and cook for another 1 minute until fragrant.
4. **Toast the Rice:**
   - Add the Arborio rice to the skillet with the onion and garlic. Stir continuously for 1-2 minutes until the rice grains are coated with oil and slightly translucent around the edges.
5. **Deglaze with Wine (if using):**
   - Pour in the white wine and stir until it is absorbed by the rice.
6. **Add Broth:**
   - Begin adding the warm broth to the skillet, one ladleful (about 1/2 cup) at a time, stirring frequently. Allow each addition of broth to be absorbed by the rice before adding the next ladleful. This process will take about 18-20 minutes. Adjust the heat as needed to maintain a gentle simmer.
7. **Incorporate Mushrooms:**
   - About halfway through adding the broth, stir in the sautéed mushrooms.
8. **Finish the Risotto:**
   - Continue adding broth and stirring until the rice is creamy and cooked al dente, with a slight bite to it. You may not need to use all of the broth; the amount can vary depending on the rice and desired consistency.
9. **Add Parmesan Cheese:**
   - Stir in the grated Parmesan cheese until it melts and combines into the risotto. Season with salt and pepper to taste.
10. **Serve:**

- Remove the mushroom risotto from heat. Serve immediately, garnished with chopped fresh parsley if desired. Enjoy the creamy and flavorful mushroom risotto as a main dish or as a side!

Tips:

- Mushroom Variation: Feel free to use a mix of different mushrooms for added depth of flavor.
- Creaminess: For an extra creamy texture, you can stir in a tablespoon of butter or a splash of heavy cream at the end of cooking.
- Leftovers: Mushroom risotto can thicken upon standing. To reheat leftovers, add a splash of broth or water and gently heat while stirring until warmed through and creamy again.

This mushroom risotto recipe is a comforting and elegant dish that's perfect for a cozy dinner at home. Enjoy the rich flavors and creamy texture of this classic Italian favorite!

www.ingramcontent.com/pod-product-compliance
Lightning Source LLC
LaVergne TN
LVHW061947070526
838199LV00060B/4009